ASHE Higher Education Report: Volume 32, Number 4
Kelly Ward, Lisa E. Wolf-Wendel, Series Editors

Intergroup Dialogue in Higher Education: Meaningful Learning About Social Justice

Ximena Zúñiga
Biren (Ratnesh) A. Nagda
Mark Chesler
Adena Cytron-Walker

Intergroup Dialogue in Higher Education: Meaningful Learning About
Social Justice
Ximena Zúñiga, Biren (Ratnesh) A. Nagda, Mark Chesler, Adena Cytron-Walker
ASHE Higher Education Report: Volume 32, Number 4
Kelly Ward, Lisa E. Wolf-Wendel, Series Editors

ISSN 1551-6970   electronic ISSN 1554-6306   ISBN 978-0-7879-9579-9

The ASHE Higher Education Report is part of the Jossey-Bass Higher and Adult
Education Series and is published six times a year by Wiley Subscription Services,
Inc., A Wiley Company, at Jossey-Bass, 989 Market Street, San Francisco,
California 94103-1741.

For subscription information, see the Back Issue/Subscription Order Form
in the back of this volume.

CALL FOR PROPOSALS: Prospective authors are strongly encouraged to contact
Kelly Ward (kaward@wsu.edu) or Lisa Wolf-Wendel (lwolf@ku.edu). See "About
the ASHE Higher Education Report Series" in the back of this volume.

Visit the Jossey-Bass Web site at **www.josseybass.com.**

Advisory Board

The ASHE Higher Education Report Series is sponsored by the Association for the Study of Higher Education (ASHE), which provides an editorial advisory board of ASHE members.

Contents

Executive Summary

This volume outlines the theory, practice, and research on intergroup dialogue (IGD). Intergroup dialogue is a face-to-face, interactive, and facilitated learning experience that brings together twelve to eighteen students from two or more social identity groups over a sustained period to explore commonalities and differences, examine the nature and consequences of systems of power and privilege, and find ways to work together to promote social justice. Some groups that participate in intergroup dialogue include men and women; white people and people of color; African Americans and Latinos or Latinas; heterosexuals, gay men, lesbians, bisexual and transgender people; and Christians and Jews. Students engage in active and experiential learning over the course of eight to twelve sessions. The IGD groups are guided by trained facilitators who use an educational curriculum. Intergroup dialogues are offered in a variety of ways on different campuses, ranging from cocurricular activities to full-fledged courses.

Over the past decade, intergroup dialogue has evolved as a sought-after practice in higher education for fostering learning and building mutual understanding among students from different social backgrounds (Hurtado, Milem, Clayton-Pedersen, and Allen, 1999; President's Initiative on Race Advisory Board, 1998). This practice has its roots in the progressive democratic education and intergroup education movements of the 1930s and 1940s. Intergroup dialogue shares common goals with other diversity education efforts in higher education, yet it is distinctive in its critical-dialogic approach to addressing issues of social identity and social location in the context of systems of power and privilege. Unlike efforts that emphasize content knowledge about group inequality or prejudice reduction through personalized encounters, intergroup dialogue strives to balance intimate, interactive, and reflective encounters among diverse participants with cognitive, affective, and active approaches to learning about diversity and social justice (Nagda and Derr, 2004; Schoem and Hurtado, 2001; Zúñiga and Nagda, 1993a; Zúñiga, Nagda, and Sevig, 2002).

What Are the Goals of Intergroup Dialogue?

The specific goals of intergroup dialogue are to:

Promote the development of consciousness about social identity and social group differences by examining how personal and group-related attitudes, relationships with other people and groups, information about the social world, and access to critical social and material resources are shaped by systems of power and privilege;

Help members of social identity groups with a history of conflict or potential conflict to forge connections across differences and conflicts by building caring and reciprocal relationships that support the development of mutual empathy in an inclusive environment where participants can learn to listen and speak openly, engage with one another seriously, take risks, explore differences and conflicts, and discover common ground; and

Strengthen individual and collective capacities for social action by fostering connections and alliances across and in social identity groups and build the confidence, commitment, and skills needed to support coalitional actions for social justice inside and outside the dialogues.

As a whole, the educational goals of intergroup dialogue—consciousness raising, building relationships across differences and conflicts, and strengthening individual and collective capacities to promote social justice—fulfill the call for college graduates to have the knowledge, commitment, and skills essential for living and working in a diverse and socially stratified society (Guarasci and Cornwell, 1997; Gurin, 1999; hooks, 1994, 2003; Schoem and Hurtado, 2001).

How Are Intergroup Dialogues Structured and Designed?

To promote a sense of equal status in the group (Allport, 1954; Pettigrew, 1998), participants in an intergroup dialogue are drawn in equal numbers from the social identity groups participating in the dialogue. Trained cofacilitators, one from each group participating in the dialogue, facilitate dialogic engagement and provide a model for working across differences.

To successfully meet the goals of intergroup dialogue, participants must gain knowledge about intergroup issues and conflicts, critically reflect on their own social identities and locations, and actively engage in honest and fruitful dialogue. In contrast to the banking approach to education (Freire, 1970), intergroup dialogue relies on student-centered pedagogies that assume that students can cocreate knowledge through facilitated active learning processes that value learning from experience as well as from conceptual frameworks, literature, empirical data, and story telling (Adams, 1997; Brookfield and Preskill, 1999, 2005; hooks, 1994, 2003; Stage, Muller, Kinzie, and Simmons, 1998; Wink, 2005).

Participants are encouraged to address constructively the often-hidden and -contested territories of social identity and intergroup relations through an educational design that explicitly attends to both content concerns (*what* participants talk about and learn) and process concerns (*how* participants engage with each other and with learning). This process is accomplished by intentionally weaving structured activities and dialogic methods that encourage individual and collective learning. Because critical and reflective conversations across differences do not occur naturally or easily in a society that is divided and socially stratified along social identity–group lines, intergroup dialogue uses a four-stage curricular design that moves from group beginnings to exploring differences and commonalities to addressing controversial issues to considering or taking actions for social justice. Three practice principles— balancing and integrating personal and structural levels of analysis, exploring commonalities and differences, and linking reflection and action— inform the educational design and guide the work of intergroup dialogue facilitators.

Who Facilitates Intergroup Dialogues and What Are Their Roles and Responsibilities?

In intergroup dialogue, facilitation means active, responsive guidance, not formal instruction. An important role of facilitators is to enable the group to develop its own processes and ways of gaining knowledge. Rather than simply presenting data, concepts, and theories, facilitators engage individual participants and the group in reflecting, sharing, and dialoguing about perspectives, feelings, and desires that are both personally and socially relevant. Facilitators support and challenge participants to maximize their learning rather than evaluate individual participants against preestablished performance criteria. They are coparticipants, not experts, in the dialogue process.

Facilitators participate in training activities and are provided with ongoing coaching and support while facilitating the intergroup dialogue. Preparing competent facilitators requires recruiting people who are ready to learn and use the knowledge, awareness, and skills required to understand and work with the distinctive features of intergroup dialogue. A few intergroup dialogue programs have used faculty as facilitators, but it is more common for student affairs staff to serve in this capacity. On a few campuses, graduate or undergraduate students serve as trained peer facilitators for other graduate or undergraduate students.

What Is the Impact of Intergroup Dialogue on Participants and What Accounts for the Impact?

The promise of intergroup dialogue is supported by a growing body of quantitative and qualitative studies conducted by researchers and practitioners of intergroup dialogue (Gurin, 1999; Hurtado, 2001; Stephan and Stephan, 2001). This research suggests that intergroup dialogue has a positive effect on student outcomes that is directly related to the educational goals of raising participants' consciousness, building relationships across differences and conflicts, and strengthening individual and collective capacities to promote social justice (Gurin, Peng, Lopez, and Nagda, 1999; Lopez, Gurin, and Nagda, 1998; Nagda, Kim, Moise-Swanson, and Kim, 2006; Zúñiga, 2004). Moreover, specific communication and pedagogical processes (such as sustained and intimate engagement across differences and a focus on both cognitive and affective dimensions of dialogue and learning) appear to support the development of these student outcomes (Nagda, 2006; Nagda, Kim, and Truelove, 2004; Nagda and Zúñiga, 2003; Yeakley, 1998). Further research is needed to determine more precisely what and how students learn in intergroup dialogue and how the practice can be improved.

How Are Intergroup Dialogues Organized on Campus and What Is Their Institutional Impact?

Intergroup dialogue has garnered increasing interest from faculty, student affairs professionals, students, and administrators over the last decade. It provides a forum for addressing issues that many feel are too controversial to examine effectively in the classroom and to encourage a learning process that enables significant collaboration among faculty, student affairs professionals, and student facilitators.

Several paths lead to creation of dialogue programs in higher education. Be it an independent, student-generated effort or housed in student or academic affairs, its adaptability to a range of situations makes it appealing to students, staff, faculty, and administrators from varying parts of the campus. Intergroup dialogue programs share common goals and design features, though each individual program is tailored to the specific objectives and needs of the campus, academic department, or student affairs unit it serves.

Although the institutional impact of intergroup dialogue remains an area of further research and inquiry, these programs appear to yield valuable institutional benefits on many campuses. Both students and faculty report that students transfer the skills learned to other areas of their lives on campus—student leadership positions, for example—and faculty and student affairs professionals have found that being involved in intergroup dialogue has enhanced their work on other areas, including the classroom. As colleges and universities weigh different approaches for promoting citizens' engagement in a diverse democracy, they may find that intergroup dialogue offers a fruitful and exciting opportunity for faculty, student affairs professionals, and students to work together to build a more inclusive and just future.

Foreword

The educational value of diversity was the major theme of the seventy-four amicus briefs submitted on behalf of the University of Michigan in defending its use of race-conscious admissions policies in cases that were acted on by the Supreme Court in June 2003. These briefs—from the nonprofit and corporate sectors to professional organizations to the military—stressed, in language unique to their particular societal missions, the crucial importance of students' acquiring an understanding of different life experiences and group perspectives and developing the cultural competence that will be needed to be effective leaders in the United States and the world. The Supreme Court ruling affirmed the use of race-conscious admissions. We, as scholars and professionals in higher education, must now grapple with the question *What kind of academic experiences will promote outcomes toward cultural competence?*

Intergroup dialogue, as conceptualized and described in this volume, explicitly engages students in the cognitive, emotional, and skill development that cultural competence demands. Learning how to talk and listen across differences and to discern commonalities as well as differences in these interactions is fundamental to cultural understanding and intercultural competence. So, too, are appreciating the life experiences of people from backgrounds distinct from one's own, understanding the dynamics of inequalities, and learning to work with conflicts that inevitably emerge in intercultural situations. Together, all these outcomes augur well for working cooperatively across differences in the pursuit of equality and social justice.

The authors, who collectively created intergroup dialogue nearly two decades ago, have written the definitive statement of its development and current status in higher education. This volume is a treasure trove of theory, research, and practice that will guide scholars and practitioners in student affairs for years to come as they increasingly seek effective tools to actualize the educational potential of diversity.

Patricia Gurin
University of Michigan
Ann Arbor

Acknowledgments

Our professional involvement with intergroup dialogue started at the University of Michigan. Ximena Zúñiga was the original director of the Program on Intergroup Relations where intergroup dialogue originated in 1988. Biren (Ratnesh) A. Nagda started his work with the program as a teaching assistant for the program's introductory course. Zúñiga and Nagda, with Todd Sevig, developed the intergroup dialogue model. Zúñiga has introduced intergroup dialogue to the undergraduate experience at the University of Massachusetts Amherst and directs a theory-research-practice sequence on intergroup dialogue that prepares graduate students in social justice education to lead intergroup dialogue in K–16 settings. Nagda has infused intergroup dialogue in social work education at the University of Washington, where he directs the Intergroup Dialogue, Education and Action (IDEA) Center that supports campus- and community-wide intergroup dialogue facilitation training, curriculum development, and evaluation. Mark Chesler was among the founding faculty of the Program on Intergroup Relations and is actively involved in the training of undergraduate peer intergroup dialogue facilitators at the University of Michigan. Adena Cytron-Walker, an undergraduate student at Michigan, participated in intergroup dialogue and served as a facilitator. She furthered her interest in intergroup dialogue as a graduate student and coordinator of undergraduate intergroup dialogue courses at the University of Massachusetts Amherst.

This book grew out of a desire to capture our learning about intergroup dialogue over the last eighteen years and to share with others, in one volume, the knowledge we have gained from our practice and research in this area.

This manuscript was conceptualized collectively. Each of us provided leadership in drafting one or more chapters, usually working in pairs, and we each read and critiqued all the chapters. Biren (Ratnesh) A. Nagda took the primary responsibility for conceptualizing and writing "Research on Outcomes and Processes of Intergroup Dialogue."

Numerous people have shared our interest in intergroup dialogue theory, practice, and research. We especially would like to acknowledge David Schoem, Patricia Gurin, Luis Sfeir-Younis, Andrea Monroe, Pamela Motoike, Todd Sevig, Genevieve Stewart, Monita Thompson, Anne Martinez, John Diamond, Anna Yeakley, and Carolyn Vasques-Scalera. They all contributed to the development of intergroup dialogues in the early years of the program at the University of Michigan.

We also thank Jane Mildred, Mary McClintock, Jaclyn Rodriguez, Alina Torres, Elaine Whitlock, and our anonymous reviewers for their thoughtful and helpful feedback on earlier drafts of this monograph. We express our deep appreciation for our valued colleagues—Maurianne Adams, James A. Banks, Lee Ann Bell, Bailey W. Jackson, Tanya Kachwaha, Barbara Love, Sylvia Hurtado, Kelly Maxwell, Patricia Romney, Beverly Tatum, Walter Stephan, Jesus Treviño, and Edwina Uehara—who have strongly supported intergroup dialogues over so many years.

Most of all, we thank the many other colleagues, intergroup dialogue participants, and facilitators who have helped to make intergroup dialogues in higher education a meaningful approach to learning about social justice.

Published online in Wiley InterScience
(www.interscience.wiley.com) • DOI: 10.1002/aehe.3204

Intergroup Dialogue in Higher Education: Definition, Origins, and Practices

INTERGROUP DIALOGUE IS AN INNOVATIVE PRACTICE IN higher education that promotes student engagement across cultural and social divides, fostering learning about social diversity and inequalities and cultivating an ethos of social responsibility. This approach to diversity education on college and university campuses responds to a growing need for educational practices that prepares students to live, work, and lead in a complex, diverse, and stratified society (Banks, 2002; Chesler, Lewis, and Crowfoot, 2005; Guarasci and Cornwell, 1997; Gurin, 1999; hooks, 1994; Hurtado, Milem, Clayton-Pedersen, and Allen, 1999; Sleeter and McLaren, 1995; Stephan and Stephan, 2001; Schoem, Frankel, Zúñiga, and Lewis, 1993; Tatum, 1997).

Intergroup dialogue (IGD), the focus of this monograph, is one of several dialogue and deliberation practices currently being used on college and university campuses in the United States. Many of these practices seek to foster conversation about contentious issues in collaborative ways (Schoem and others, 2001; Zúñiga and Nagda, 2001). One model, Study Circles (Flavin-McDonald and Barrett, 1999; McCoy and Sherman, 1994; McCoy and McCormick, 2001), emphasizes community building and social action. Study Circles bring community members together in small groups to build relationships, deliberate about community issues, and explore actions to effect change in their communities (also see http://www.studycircles.org). Another model, Sustained Dialogue (Parker, 2006; Saunders, 1999, 2003), draws from work in international conflict resolution and peace building. In Sustained Dialogue, students of diverse backgrounds come together to build mutual respect, identify issues of conflict, and generate action plans, including workable agreements to conflicts or disputes (also see *http://www.sustaineddialogue.org*). We focus on intergroup dialogue in this monograph for several reasons. First, intergroup dialogue is the only approach to campus dialogue that originated and was developed on college and university campuses. Other approaches to dialogue and deliberation have been adapted for campus use but were initially developed as community-based interventions. Because of its roots in higher education, intergroup dialogue is grounded in the theories, knowledge, research, and pedagogical principles drawn from the scholarship of teaching and learning. The intergroup dialogue approach has also been more systematically researched than any other campus-based dialogue practice. Finally, the authors of this monograph were among those who originally designed and developed intergroup dialogue at the University of Michigan and are among those now implementing intergroup dialogue programs at other institutions of higher learning. Thus, our presentation and discussion of intergroup dialogue in this monograph is informed by our own accumulated knowledge, experience, and scholarship in this area.

Defining Intergroup Dialogue

Intergroup dialogue is a distinct approach to dialogue across differences in higher education. It can be broadly defined as a face-to-face facilitated learning experience that brings together students from different social identity groups over a sustained period of time to understand their commonalities and differences, examine the nature and impact of societal inequalities, and explore ways of working together toward greater equality and justice.

Intergroup dialogue was developed in the 1980s at the University of Michigan–Ann Arbor during a period of racial strife and conflict on many college campuses in the United States. It is now being implemented at a number of colleges and universities around the country. On some campuses, intergroup dialogues are stand-alone cocurricular activities, but at others, they are offered as part of a course in psychology, sociology, education, communication, or social work. IGD programs are currently operating at a number of institutions, including Arizona State University; Bucknell University; Mount

Holyoke College; Occidental College; Portland Community College; Spelman College; Syracuse University; University of California, San Diego; University of Illinois at Urbana-Champaign; University of Maryland, College Park; University of Massachusetts Amherst; University of Michigan, Ann Arbor; University of New Hampshire; University of Texas at Austin; University of Vermont; and University of Washington, Seattle (see Schoem and Hurtado, 2001, for descriptions of selected programs).

Intergroup dialogue brings together twelve to eighteen people from two or more social identity groups: men and women; white people, biracial/multiracial/ethnic people, and people of color; blacks, Latinos/as, and Native Americans; Arabs and Jews; lesbians, gay men, bisexual and heterosexual people; people from working-, middle-, and upper-socioeconomic class backgrounds; and Christians, Muslims, and Jews. These meetings are supported and guided by a skilled team of cofacilitators that use an educational curriculum integrating cognitive, affective, and behavioral dimensions of learning. The cofacilitators are chosen to reflect the composition of the dialogue; for example, a dialogue involving men and women would have one male and one female cofacilitator.

Intergroup dialogue is marked by its *critical-dialogic* approach to exploring commonalities and differences in and between social identity groups, its reliance on *sustained communication and involvement* to bridge differences and move participants to deeper and more meaningful levels of engagement, and its *intergroup focus.* By recognizing the centrality of social group affiliation based on race, gender, sexual orientation, religion, and other socially constructed categories, intergroup dialogue fosters a critical examination of the impact of power relations and social inequality on intergroup relations (Nagda and others, 1999; Zúñiga and Nagda, 2001).

Intergroup dialogue is grounded in the assumptions that interpersonal and cross-group relations on campus are affected by the histories and current realities of intergroup conflict in the United States and that these conflicts must be explored through *dialogic* encounters. In contrast to "banking" approaches to diversity education in which the teacher-expert deposits knowledge into students as if they were empty vessels waiting to be filled (Freire, 1970), dialogic interaction promotes active, generative, and transformative connections and explorations among participants and between participants and facilitators. Intergroup dialogue recognizes the importance of listening and speaking honestly and openly to encourage shared meaning and improved interpersonal communication and relationships (Ellinor and Gerard, 1998; Weiler, 1994).

Communication flows in many directions as thoughts and feelings are shared and questions and issues are posed for everyone to consider. Dialogue involves "periods of lots of noise as people share and lots of silence as people muse" (Wink, 2005, p. 41). Different from "mere talk" or casual conversations, dialogue is an intentional, facilitated process that has a focus and a purpose (Brookfield and Preskill, 2005; Chesler, Lewis, and Crowfoot, 2005; Romney, 2003). Dialogue differs from debate, where one party tries to convince the other party (or an audience) of the correctness of his or her own position as well as the incorrectness of the other position. Dialogue, unlike debate, builds a relationship between participants that engages the heart as well as the intellect (Huang-Nissen, 1999; Romney, 2003).

Communication across social identity–based differences can be emotionally difficult, and tensions may develop between participants as they explore their differing experiences and the social and historical forces that divide them. Working through these tensions and achieving understanding require *sustained communication and involvement,* not just a one-time workshop or event. Intergroup dialogue requires a series of eight to twelve structured, facilitated meetings to promote meaningful dialogue and learning and to build relationships over time.

The emphasis on interpersonal communication and learning is expanded in intergroup dialogue to include an *intergroup focus* that recognizes that members of social identity groups have different locations in systems of advantage and disadvantage. Unequal social statuses, which have influenced participants' past perceptions and experiences and their groups' histories and present opportunities and access to resources, also affect interpersonal relationships. The relationships between the groups, not just the individuals, participating in the intergroup dialogue are addressed as participants work through conflict and critically examine the cultural, political, and economic bases of institutionalized discrimination and privilege. Participants in intergroup dialogue do not simply learn about the sociopolitical environment in which their social identity groups interact; they also develop a critical analytic perspective on why these environments exist and operate in the way they do and who benefits and suffers from these arrangements. This critical examination encourages participants to take action to change these societal structures as a necessary condition for the improvement of relationships among social groups and individuals.

In summary, the focus on sustained communication about intergroup issues from a critical-dialogic perspective differentiates intergroup dialogue from other diversity education efforts that emphasize, for example, content assimilation about contemporary race or gender relations in the United States. It is also distinct from curricular activities that promote intergroup communication without explicitly addressing power relations or problem-solving workshops that seek to identify strategies to address specific conflicts or interest group issues. Thus, intergroup dialogue integrates cognitive learning about identity, difference, and inequality with affective involvement of oneself and others through sharing intimate personal reflections and meaningful critical dialogues.

Historical Roots of and Contemporary Influences on Intergroup Dialogue

Intergroup dialogue has its roots in philosophical and cultural traditions that have valued dialogue as a method of communication and inquiry (Zúñiga and Nagda, 2001). These traditions gave rise to the democratic, experiential education, and intergroup education movements of the last century (McGee Banks, 2005; Stephan and Stephan, 2001; Zúñiga, Nagda, and Sevig, 2002). Dialogue as a communication practice has been used in many cultural and discourse traditions to support inquiry and explore shared concerns.

The practice of dialogue in education can be traced to the progressive democratic education movement inspired by the work of John Dewey and other influential educators working at Teachers College during the 1930s and 1940s. These educational pioneers conceptualized dialogue as the practice of deliberative democracy and sought to foster in learners the capacity and disposition to participate in such deliberations (Burbules, 2000). Dewey believed that "the theory and practice of democracy should be nourished by the power of pedagogy" (Wink, 2005, p. 106). Democratic educators, by offering students the opportunity to work on real situations and problems, stimulated reflection on the real world (Brockbank and McGill, 2000). Citizenship education and learner-centered pedagogies and experiential learning methods are legacies of this movement (Adams, 1997; Banks, 2004). For instance, Paulo Freire, Myles Horton, and others applied many of Dewey's ideas in the popular education movement in an effort to empower marginalized peoples to challenge social inequities in the United States and other societies (Horton and Freire, 1990). More recently, critical theorists have questioned Dewey's idea that dialogue as a form of communication can by itself foster democratic practices in a liberal democracy. From this perspective, Habermas (1981) argues that because democracy is an "unfinished project" marked by cultural and status differences, the preservation of the democratic process requires the development of speech situations that allow people to communicate across differences to reshape prevailing power relations (Morrow and Torres, 2002). Freire's writings (1970) about dialogue as a liberatory educational practice have influenced the work of critical, feminist, and antiracist theorists in education (hooks, 1994; Sleeter and McLaren, 1995; Weiler, 1993).

The intergroup education movement of the 1940s and 1950s also influenced efforts aimed at bridging differences across social identity groups. Intergroup education drew from Allport's conditions for positive intergroup contact—equal status, acquaintance potential, and interdependency (Allport, 1954; Pettigrew, 1998). This movement grew out of the social unrest following the U.S. "great migration," when large numbers of African Americans from the South moved to industrial cities in the North. Parallel efforts took place in the Southwest in response to the large migration of Mexican Americans after World War II (Castañeda, 2004). Intergroup education is also considered a precursor to contemporary practices oriented toward antibias, antiracist, multicultural, or social justice education (Adams, 1997; McGee Banks, 2005).

Two approaches to multicultural education rooted in intergroup education—a human relations approach and education that is multicultural and social reconstructionist—have also influenced intergroup dialogue theory and practice (Sleeter and Grant, 1999). Although intergroup dialogue is not strictly aligned with either approach, it draws elements from both. The human relations approach, focused on intergroup understanding and harmony, aims to improve relationships between groups through personalization, building acquaintances and friendships, and engaging in cooperative projects. These educational activities and processes may reduce individual prejudice but are not directed toward greater social justice and addressing inequalities. In contrast, education that is critical, multicultural, and social reconstructionist, such as social justice education, holds central the analysis of social inequalities and the role members of both privileged and disadvantaged groups can take in creating change (Adams, Bell, and Griffin, 1997; Sleeter and Grant, 1999).

In reconciling the tension between approaches that emphasize fostering positive intergroup relations and those that emphasize critical understanding of social inequalities, intergroup dialogue draws from two other sources in articulating its specific pedagogical practices. First, work in conflict transformation and peace building (Norman, 1991, 1994; Lederach, 1995; Saunders, 1999, 2003) provides important lessons that are incorporated into intergroup dialogue (for example, building collaborative ties among conflicting parties in small-group contexts). Although conflicts in communication, perceptions, and understanding across differences are located in larger systems of social inequality, conflict transformation practitioners foster collaborative ties to promote more equal and just relationships among participating groups. Thus, participants explore individual or group actions aimed at transforming their intergroup hostilities with the goal of changing unjust situations. Second, feminist pedagogy (hooks, 1994; Romney, Tatum, and Jones, 1992; Schniedewind, 1992) and social justice education theory and practice (Adams, Bell, and Griffin, 1997) have centered on the integration of content and process in teaching and learning about social justice issues. In intergroup dialogue, for example, although understanding systems of inequalities and ways of challenging those inequalities is critical, attention also is focused on understanding and articulating how the process of learning about such knowledge is designed and facilitated to foster self and collective awareness, affective ties, and social justice commitments.

Organization of This Monograph

This introductory chapter has introduced intergroup dialogue, its historical roots, its location among similar diversity education practices, and its core components. The subsequent chapters provide readers with a detailed discussion about theory, practice, and research on intergroup dialogue as well as information needed to implement an IGD program on the college campus.

The next chapter, "Educational Goals of Intergroup Dialogue," describes the three core educational goals of intergroup dialogue as a critical-dialogic practice—consciousness raising, relationship building across differences and conflict, and strengthening individual and collective capacities to promote social justice—and discusses the constitutive elements of each goal. "Design and Practice Principles in Intergroup Dialogue" presents the design elements and practice principles that guide the enactment of these goals. "Facilitating Intergroup Dialogues" builds on the previous two chapters and focuses on facilitation in intergroup dialogue. It describes the importance of cofacilitation and the role of facilitators as well as their requisite competencies and training. It also discusses the particular challenges that IGD facilitators face in their work. "Research on Outcomes and Processes of Intergroup Dialogue" reviews current research on the educational benefits of intergroup dialogue, highlighting the range of outcomes and factors that influence achieving those outcomes. It also proposes areas of further research. "Program Development, Implementation, and Institutional Impact" discusses issues to address in developing and implementing dialogue programs on college campuses as well as their institutional impact. After a brief conclusion, the monograph presents an appendix of educational resources that includes structured activities and methods to foster intergroup dialogue and learning about social identity and social inequality and tools to support the training of facilitators in intergroup dialogue.

Educational Goals
of Intergroup Dialogue

INTERGROUP DIALOGUE IS A CRITICAL-DIALOGICAL APPROACH that integrates three core educational goals: consciousness raising, building relationships across differences and conflicts, and strengthening individual and collective capacities to promote social justice. These goals provide a conceptual framework for the design and practice of intergroup dialogue. This chapter describes each of these goals, its philosophical and pedagogical roots, and its use in IGD efforts.

Consciousness Raising

Although this goal draws from the work of Freire (1970) and others, consciousness raising has a specific meaning in the context of intergroup dialogue. Consciousness raising has been thought of as an educational process by which members of oppressed groups come to understand the history and circumstances of their oppression. But intergroup dialogue aims at raising the consciousness of all participants, not only those who are members of the less-advantaged groups. For a genuine dialogue to occur, it is just as important for members of privileged groups to understand how they and others have been affected by privilege as it is for members of less-advantaged groups to understand how they have been affected by subordination. All participants need to grapple with understanding their own social identity group's history, involvement in patterns of privilege or oppression, and the impact of this history on themselves and others. Members of both advantaged and disadvantaged groups must gain a deeper understanding of each other's situations and grapple with effects of privilege and subordination on their relationships (Collins, 1993). This kind of consciousness raising occurs in individuals and groups and between groups. Eventually, everyone must learn that "the 'we' that's in trouble is all of us" (Johnson, 2001, p. 9).

Moreover, all people are members of several different social identity groups, some of which place them in positions of privilege (in the United States, for example, being white, male, owning or upper class, Christian, and heterosexual) and others that place them in positions of disadvantage (being a person of color, female, a member of a lower economic class, a religious minority, or gay). In dialogues, participants are encouraged to recognize their multiple identities and the relationships among them while focusing on one particular identity to intentionally explore a particular line of intergroup difference. For instance, in a gender dialogue, participants primarily focus on gender relationships while acknowledging the influence of other group identities such as race and ethnicity or sexual orientation. In a race/ethnicity dialogue, members of each group also examine intragroup differences in gender, religion, class, or sexual orientation. These within-group differences affect how members of the groups relate with one another in the intergroup dialogue as well as in the broader social context. Participants must examine these multiple identities and their relation to one another if they are to understand what it means to be a member of a socially situated identity group. Such an approach is, by definition, multidimensional and complex and strives to reflect a multicentric viewpoint (Nagda, Zúñiga, and Sevig, 1995).

The educational goal of consciousness raising in intergroup dialogue takes place through the parallel and interrelated processes of developing awareness and acquiring social system knowledge. Through discussion of readings, experiential activities, reflection, and analysis, participants are invited to explore the origins and contemporary consequences of how group differences are dealt with (for example, history, cultural heritage, social status). Participants take inventory of their experiences as members of social identity groups, examine the origins and effects of stereotypes and information or misinformation about themselves and others, and delve into the dynamics of power, privilege, and exclusion in campus and community life. The conjunction of both cognitive and affective explorations helps participants understand how and why certain patterns of intergroup dominance and subordination exist and how these patterns affect them personally. With the support of information and guided facilitation, participants are encouraged to question personal biases and preconceptions and begin to understand each other's perspectives and experiences in a larger social context.

Developing Personal and Social Identity Awareness

Theorists suggest that the process of understanding one's social identities in relation to systems of oppression such as racism and sexism generally moves from unawareness to exploration to awareness of the impact of social group membership on the self and finally toward internalizing and integrating this awareness (Bennett, Atkinson, and Rowe, 1993; Hardiman and Jackson, 1992; Helms, 1990; Tatum, 1992, 1997). This process of development is not linear. People may move back and forth between stages and may even remain in the same stage for some time. Moreover, both individuals and groups of participants often have different levels of knowledge and awareness about their own and other social identity groups and readiness to actively engage issues of social identity affiliation (Zúñiga, Vasques-Scalera, Sevig, and Nagda, 1996). For example, participants from privileged social identity groups typically report knowing less about the ramifications or impact of their own group membership on others than do people of disadvantaged groups (Zúñiga, Nagda, and Sevig, 2002).

In the process of developing awareness at multiple levels, participants become clearer and more reflective about the meaning of their social identities and their groups' relationships with other groups. Intergroup dialogue acknowledges the centrality of understanding social identity group memberships in light of each group's history and contemporary status. Participants are challenged to consider certain questions: What does it mean to be a member of a specific social identity group? How is who we are shaped by our socialization into specific social statuses in society? How do we benefit from certain identities, and how are we limited or constrained by others? How do we relate to social identity groups that are differentially situated from us? Intergroup dialogue uses both personal and sociopolitical lenses to examine such questions by engaging participants in developing personal awareness, group awareness, and awareness of the privileges and disadvantages of group membership in a variety of contexts.

Social System Knowledge

Consciousness raising also requires the awareness that membership in a social group is only one factor influencing how people see the world. Indeed, individuals' experiences of social inequality and injustice are influenced by their intellectual understanding of the dynamics of social oppression and vice versa. Relationships between groups and the respective statuses of groups in the larger society are shaped and affected by interpersonal, institutional, and societal privilege and power dynamics as well as the groups' histories and present environment. Participants are challenged to consider how the relationship between the social identity groups has been shaped by history and by economic systems and how the relationship continues to be reinforced and reproduced by social institutions and institutional barriers. Increased knowledge of social systems helps participants clarify the meaning and scope of prejudice, discrimination, and oppression and explore the institutional web of discrimination that reinforces the dynamics of power and privilege in educational, judicial, and economic systems. By explicitly attending to social identity at the personal level, patterns of conflict or collaboration at the intergroup level, and systems of inequality at the societal level, participants are often able to see some of the ways systems of oppression (racism, sexism, classism, or heterosexism) shape people's lives. Gradually they may understand that the conflicts in perceptions, tensions, and misunderstandings that surface between individuals and between different social identity groups do not happen in a vacuum or randomly but are a result of the historical and institutional dynamics of privilege and disadvantage.

Building Relationships Across Differences and Conflicts

A second educational goal of intergroup dialogue focuses on building relationships between and among participants from two or more social identity groups with a history of estrangement or conflict. Because intergroup dialogue focuses on people's learning as individuals *and* as members of social identity groups, the ways that participants interact and relate with each other are important. A key feature of relationship building is the explicit recognition that relationships in the dialogue group are likely to be affected by the asymmetrical relationships and history of conflict or potential conflicts between the social identity groups involved (Maoz, 2001). Consequently, intergroup dialogue focuses on how relationships occur among people in full recognition of their social group identities. Forging relationships across differences is encouraged through building the capacity for sustained communication and bridging differences.

Building Capacity for Sustained Communication

Members of different groups may come to the dialogic encounter with different and often conflicting knowledge, experiences, and goals. For instance, Duster (1991) reports that white participants often enter intergroup communications with a desire to get to know other people and to build contacts. Participants of color, on the other hand, often enter such conversations with an eye toward getting support for concerted action to alter systems of discrimination and oppression. Under such circumstances, members of privileged groups often report feeling confused about the anger expressed (sometimes toward them) by members of disadvantaged groups in the dialogue. They may feel naive about the realities of life experienced by members of disadvantaged groups and feel innocent of responsibility for their own and others' location in systems of oppression. On the other hand, participants from less-privileged social groups may be disturbed by the limited knowledge that privileged group members have about particular forms of oppression.

Such encounters can easily turn into polarizing debates that seek advantage or conversion or polite conversations that avoid talking about differences or difficult issues. Intergroup dialogue differs fundamentally from polarizing communication (like policy debates) or mere talk, neither of which promotes meaningful communication. It also differs from one-time training sessions and single in-depth encounters that do not offer sustained contact. Unlike these common variants of intergroup communication and learning, the IGD model relies on extended meetings among participants to develop deeper intergroup understanding (even if it is about why there is conflict between the groups), mutual respect, and empathic connection between participants. As participants continue to listen to each other's experiences and perspectives (even conflictual perspectives) over time, they can think through issues together. Because intergroup dialogue is not an event or an isolated encounter but a process that takes place over time, it can create an open space in which people can engage with one another honestly and seriously with a desire to understand and care rather than to win or lose. Moreover, multisession, sustained, face-to-face dialogic communication fosters deeper levels of mutual understanding across lines of difference. By actively listening to one another, sharing personal experiences and views, asking and answering difficult questions, and questioning each other's ideas and beliefs, participants in intergroup dialogue gain perspective into each other's worlds and explore the social context in which they live.

Moving from polite (or impolite) interactions to meaningful engagement can be challenging and frustrating. Creating a conducive climate for learning across differences requires a group environment that supports building relationships in the here and now. It also requires a process that challenges and overcomes patterns of intergroup communication that reflect only, or primarily, the dominant group's norms and styles. By using dialogic methods such as speaking and listening activities and talking circles, participants gradually develop the capacity to listen attentively to each other, talk openly and honestly, appreciate different perspectives, and ask naive or politically incorrect questions. Through planned and sequentially structured activities that provide participants with experiences that increase in difficulty, intensity, and intimacy, relationships are built as the curriculum unfolds. These experiences occur in a structured and bounded (by membership, guidelines, time, and space) environment. Schoem and others (2001) note that trust in this type of group process grows and is tested as dialogue participants feel freer and more confident to raise difficult questions, challenge each other, express anger, offer support, and continue the conversation.

Bridging Differences

The development of relationships across and within social identity groups offers more than just an opportunity for people from different social identity groups to come together and learn about each other. Unlike feel-good types of cross-group encounters that attempt to promote understanding by avoiding, masking, or overcoming conflicts, intergroup dialogue recognizes that communicating about and, if possible, working through conflict are both positive and necessary parts of the intergroup encounter. Such disagreements and conflicts can become valuable opportunities for participants to engage in significant conversations about different perspectives and tensions shaping their relationships.

Given that participants from the social identity groups participating in an intergroup dialogue come from different societal locations and experiences, they may slip into traditional dysfunctional patterns of conversation and interaction in which (1) privileged group members express their goodwill and sense of innocence, ask many questions, and retreat into silence when questioned or challenged; (2) privileged group members deny any responsibility for the impact of their accumulated advantages on others; (3) disadvantaged group members feel (or are made to feel) responsible for educating members of privileged groups and feel constrained to defend their group from what may be perceived as hostile or naive questioning; (4) disadvantaged group members fail to look beyond their sense of oppression to acknowledge problems in their own communities or potential advantages of group membership; (5) all parties try to rank their own or others' oppression; and (6) no one seeks alliances with anyone. These patterns are all sources of immediate conflict among dialogue participants, but they also constitute an agenda for learning. Examining such patterns of interactions can help participants discover some of the intergroup dynamics shaping their relationships. If done with care and connection, even when participants' lived experience is drastically different, the IGD process can build relationships across those lines of difference.

Honest, deep, and sustained conversations about issues of social identity and social stratification inevitably shed light on the complex dynamics of connection and disconnection that result from estranged or hostile relationships between members of social groups in the larger society. Such conflicts become valuable opportunities for participants to engage in heart-to-heart conversations and to figure out new ways of thinking and relating across difference, building bridges between and among individuals across group boundaries (Zúñiga, 2003). Such bridging may occur when a white man or a man of color in a gender dialogue acknowledges his own privileged status as a man with more self-knowledge, openness, and sensitivity to the experiences shared by the women in the group and is willing to take responsibility for issues of safety and violence against women on the campus. Intragroup differences also may be bridged, for example, when a heterosexual woman of color in a dialogue about race and ethnicity who had previously challenged gay men of color for failing to participate in organizations involving students of color on campus listens attentively to their experiences with homophobia in the residence halls and asks how she could be supportive or advocate for them. Intergroup dialogue offers participants a space to experiment with such bridging behaviors as well as to cultivate confidence and commitment to continue such bridging across differences outside the dialogue setting.

Strengthening Individual and Collective Capacities to Promote Social Justice

The third educational goal of intergroup dialogue, strengthening individual and collective capacities to promote social justice, is made possible by the other two. By supporting new ways of thinking about oneself and others and the social structure in which both exist, intergroup dialogue promotes thinking about and acting for social change. The capacity to act together rests on developing commitments to fellow dialogue members and a sense of shared responsibility for challenging discrimination and creating greater justice. The process of building bridges across and within differences in social identity groups provides a structure that can empower participants to improve intergroup relations on campus and to take more responsibility for promoting equity and social justice in society at large.

Action commitments in intergroup dialogue go beyond preparing members of privileged groups to become allies with members of disadvantaged groups or empowering disadvantaged groups to enact change. Members of privileged groups can also take action on their own to counter or disown privilege, and members of less-privileged groups can forge alliances with one another. Intergroup dialogue fosters a critical understanding and enactment of alliances across differences that challenge all forms of domination and oppression. Participants are encouraged to ask questions: How do my or our actions affect others or the other group? How are my or our actions empowering or disempowering others?

Intergroup dialogue can contribute to a more socially and economically just society by graduating participants who have a commitment to social change and the skills and dispositions needed to work with other groups to make positive changes. Participants become more aware, active, critical thinkers who value their own and other people's voices. By engaging deeply with people different from themselves and by recognizing how their own identities and social locations affect themselves and others, participants learn to care about how people from both privileged and disadvantaged groups are affected by social injustice, to feel responsible for social injustice, to feel confident in their skills and abilities to develop and sustain relationships even when conflicts exist, and to feel hopeful about the possibilities of working together across differences toward a shared vision of social justice.

Toward these ends, participants in the dialogue are provided opportunities to explore actions they can take that challenge exclusion, discrimination, and institutional oppression. For example, participants are invited to examine their spheres of influence (self, friends, family, school, work, community) and identify actions they can take to intervene in unjust or hostile situations (Goodman and Schapiro, 1997). They may decide to band together with other groups to effect change, join a social justice organization on campus, take more courses on topics of identity and social justice or change, become a resident assistant to create a more inclusive intergroup climate on campus, educate members of privileged groups about their privileged location, or actively confront racism, sexism, and homophobia in their resident halls or in the local community. They can also prioritize actions and identify possible strategies and risks. Doing so moves the learning process from dialogue and reflection to visualizing actual steps to effect change. In some instances, participants practice intergroup collaboration through the planning and implementation of action projects (Zúñiga, 2004). Participating in a dialogue about these potential and real actions can help participants to reflect on the extent to which they feel ready to take action for social justice and to identify the kind of support they may need. In envisioning and then taking action, participants create opportunities to continue to learn and to carry the skills and commitments they have developed in intergroup dialogue to settings outside and beyond the dialogue.

Design and Practice Principles in Intergroup Dialogue

THIS CHAPTER DISCUSSES DESIGN ELEMENTS, the four-stage design, and core principles of practice used in intergroup dialogue to achieve the goals described in the previous chapter. It begins by outlining the pedagogical assumption that informs the IGD educational design and then highlights key design elements guiding the IGD curriculum, including the four-stage design. The chapter concludes with a discussion of three principles of practice that weave together the various design elements of intergroup dialogue.

A Key Pedagogical Assumption

The learning process in intergroup dialogue is conceived as a social process that is coconstructed and sociopolitically and historically situated (Brookfield and Preskill, 2005; Freire, 1970; hooks, 1994, 2003; Stage, Muller, Kinzie, and Simmons, 1998). In contrast to banking approaches to education, where knowledge is transmitted to students by the teacher expert, intergroup dialogue relies on student-centered pedagogies that assume students can cocreate knowledge through active learning processes that value learning from experience as well as from content materials (Lewin, 1951; Stage, Muller, Kinzie, and Simmons, 1998). Participants learn to name and describe their personal and identity-based experiences and worldviews. They use historical and conceptual frameworks to critically situate their experiences in the context of systems of power and privilege. They learn to listen and care about their relationships with others by asking questions, identifying disagreements and conflicts, and further exploring differences and commonalities in and across social identity groups.

Design Elements

In the divided and contentious society in which we live, critical and reflective dialogue between members of social identity groups does not occur naturally or easily. A well-designed educational approach is necessary if participants are to critically explore the often hidden and contested territory of social identities and intergroup relationships. Moving from polite and superficial conversations to meaningful and honest dialogue across lines of difference requires direct and active involvement by both individuals and the group. A sequential design that aligns goals, concepts, and structured activities with dialogic methods can foster individual participants' learning as well the group's development (Bell and Griffin, 1997; Brooks-Harris and Stock-Ward, 1999; Saunders, 1999; Weber, 1982). We rely on four design elements to structure the learning in intergroup dialogue: (1) sustained and intimate engagement across differences, (2) explicit attention to issues of process and content, (3) intentional selection of structured activities and dialogic methods to support both content and process, and (4) sequencing of dialogue and learning. Together these design considerations, which represent the distinctive features of intergroup dialogue, provide coherence and continuity to individual and group learning over time.

Sustained and Intimate Engagement Across Differences

Intergroup dialogue is premised on the consistent finding that for intergroup contact to be positive, it has to allow for intimate sharing over a sustained period of time (Pettigrew, 1998). Intergroup dialogue draws on many of Allport's original conditions (1954) for positive intergroup contact—equal status, acquaintance potential, and interdependency. The composition of the membership in IGD groups mirrors the social identity groups participating so as to foster a sense of equal status inside the dialogue. In intergroup dialogues we see acquaintance potential, later reconceptualized as friendship potential (Pettigrew, 1998), manifested in the personal sharing and dialoguing processes themselves (Yeakley, 1998). Students share their own experiences, listen to and learn about others, and reflect on the similarities and differences. In so doing, they move from exposure and contact to real engagement. Combining such intimacy with interdependency in learning about social inequalities and forging intergroup collaborations empowers students to build friendships and create alliances for greater social justice (Nagda, 2006).

Explicit Attention to Content and Process

Explicit attention to blending content and process is critical to support cognitive, behavioral, and affective growth when addressing issues that are both personal and sociopolitically situated (Adams, Bell, and Griffin, 1997; Beale and Schoem, 2001; Romney, Tatum, and Jones, 1992). Content typically refers to concepts, conceptual frameworks, literature, theory, empirical data, and personal stories that challenge assumptions or misinformation or stimulate questions, reflections, observations, or new behaviors (Beale and Schoem, 2001; Zúñiga, Nagda, and Sevig, 2002). Process, on the other hand, refers to the intrapersonal and interpersonal reactions, interactions, and reflections stimulated by experiential learning or exploration of controversial issues or hot topics such as immigration, reproductive rights, gay marriage and civil unions, and affirmative action. In this context, concern for process is associated with the quality of the learning process as well as the interpersonal and intergroup relationships established in the group (Beale and Schoem, 2001; Brockbank and McGill, 2000).

What (content) and how (process) participants reflect on and discuss with one another are essential to the way they generate meaning, work together to explore controversial questions, and critically examine social identity–based relations and the issues that divide them. The IGD educational design encourages participants to share their own experiences and insights (experiential content), to contextualize these experiences using materials such as relevant readings, demographic data, and conceptual frameworks to the goals of intergroup dialogue (knowledge content), and to build and actively engage in cogenerative processes with diverse peers (active learning process). All dimensions of learning—cognitive, affective, and behavioral—are woven together in an intentional IGD educational design.

Structured Activities and Dialogic Methods

The IGD design integrates structured activities and dialogic methods to support content and process learning. Structured activities help introduce concepts such as socialization, explore and reflect on experience (for example, growing up as a boy or a girl or as a white person or a person of color), and apply new knowledge and awareness to the examination of a controversial issue. Structured activities such as icebreakers, story telling, and gallery walks can support recalling and reflecting on a past or present experience; fishbowls, read-arounds, and historical timelines can help participants share and acquire new information; role plays and speaking and listening activities aid the practice of new knowledge or skills; and action plans assist in planning for application of new knowledge, awareness, or skills (Brooks-Harris and Stock-Ward, 1999). In selecting structured activities, it is helpful to consider various learning modalities and participation styles to actively support all students in the dialogue (Bell and Griffin, 1997; Brooks-Harris and Stock-Ward, 1999; Svinicki and Dixon, 1987).

Readings and conceptual organizers also help introduce new information in the dialogue. Readings can support participants' learning about a topic from various perspectives or can further challenge participants to consider experiences and perspectives other than their own. Conceptual organizers introduce concepts or frameworks for participants to use in developing specific competencies or examining their own and others' experiences in systems of advantage (Bell and Griffin, 1997). For instance, we use Bohm's building blocks of dialogue (1990)—suspending judgments, deep listening, identifying assumptions, and reflection and inquiry—as a conceptual organizer early in the educational design to help convey some of the skills involved in fruitful dialogue (see the appendix). Subsequently, we may ask participants to read Jeanne Weiler's interview of Linda Teurfs (1994), a well-known dialogue practitioner, which reviews Bohm's building blocks in preparation for the skill-building segment scheduled in the upcoming session. When addressing issues related to social identity, we offer Harro's cycle of socialization (2000b) to help participants take stock of their experiences growing up as members of a particular social identity group and to help contextualize socialized attitudes and behaviors. We may then structure a social identity–based affinity group discussion to encourage intragroup dialogue on socializing messages received while growing up as men, women, white people, or people of color. In this way, a conceptual organizer can help frame a structured activity and ground the conversation that may evolve from processing or debriefing participants' reactions to an activity.

Debriefing structured activities can stimulate inquiry, reflection, and conversation (Bell and Griffin, 1997; Brooks-Harris and Stock-Ward, 1999; Steinwachs, 1992). Dialogue methods can help unfold meaning by keeping a conversation going through deeper questioning, active listening, and connected responding (Brookfield and Preskill, 2005). Questions can help crystallize overt or covert issues by helping participants get more involved in deeper examination of emerging patterns of thoughts and feelings, and disagreements and conflicts. The kinds of questions we ask and the ways in which we ask them can make a difference in how a conversation unfolds (Brookfield and Preskill, 2005). Although some conversations may not go far, others will evolve into a "complex communal dialogue that bounces all around the room" (Palmer, 1998, p. 134). For instance, questions that ask for clarification or that encourage building on each other's comments or questions can foster mutual understanding and connected dialogue. Questions that ask for assumptions can encourage participants to articulate more explicitly the reasoning or values behind thoughts and feelings (Brookfield and Preskill, 2005) (see the appendix). Listening with the purpose of understanding can foster perspective taking and empathy and stimulate new questions that can further the conversation. It can also help participants identify common ground and points of conflict. The extent to which participants acknowledge and respond to each other's observations or questions can create "conversational momentum and continuity that may lend new meaning and purpose to discussion" (Brookfield and Preskill, 2005, p. 100).

A variety of formats can be used to structure these conversations. Dyads, small groups, and large-group discussions all help the conversations move beyond individual reflections. Other dialogic methods that help maximize participation as well as deepen the learning include "go arounds" (Silberman, 1998), "circles of voices" (Brookfield and Preskill, 2005), and "fishbowls" (see the appendix). These structures help get conversations started on a specific topic or support reflection on the experience. At certain points in the group learning, it is also helpful to build in reflections on the dialogic process itself. For instance, "dialogue about the dialogue" allows participants to discuss the quality of the conversational process, identify concerns and feelings that may be hidden or visibly troublesome such as tardiness or a few who monopolize the conversation, and perhaps set goals for improvement (see "Dialogue About the Dialogue" in the appendix).

Sequencing of Dialogue and Learning

To address issues of social identity, prejudice, and oppression, intergroup dialogue builds on the idea of sequential organizers commonly used in antibias and social justice education to introduce concepts and activities incrementally (Bell and Griffin, 1997). These organizers help pace content and process across sessions so that the overall flow makes sense to facilitators and students.

Two content-related sequential organizers are important in structuring learning about social identities and systems knowledge (Bell and Griffin, 1997). First, for individuals, *personal to institutional sequencing* confirms participants' lived and socialized experiences as valid knowledge. These personal explorations increase participants' readiness to grapple with larger institutional and system dynamics. Sharing experiences becomes the content for learning and aids further inquiry into how group affiliations and institutions such as the educational, legal, and political systems affect individual experiences. Second, for social groups, *diversity to justice sequencing* begins by attending to commonalities and differences in and across groups and proceeds to examining how they are structured by the dynamics of social inclusion or exclusion, privilege or oppression, and agency or powerlessness. The focus here is on valuing and understanding personal and social identity-based differences before proceeding to an analysis of systems of dominance, social power, and privilege that have been built around these differences. Participants are then more open to understanding that in everyday practice "difference is not neutral" (Bell and Griffin, 1997, p. 55). Kolb's phases of experiential learning—concrete experience, reflective observation, abstract conceptualization, and active experimentation (1984)—are helpful to consider in facilitating learning and dialogue along these two sequences: personal to institutional and diversity to justice. Facilitators may begin a unit or a session by asking participants to reflect on past experiences to tap into what participants already know about a topic. Then they may incorporate concepts or a discussion of an assigned reading to expand the perspectives available in the group.

Other sequential organizers help participants to negotiate the IGD experience at the affective level. *Lower- to higher-risk sequencing* takes into consideration participants' need to feel safe so they can openly engage and examine deeply held beliefs, feelings, or confusions. Such sequencing helps to pace the risk level embedded in structured activities and dialogic methods so that participants become acquainted with each other before exploring difficult and controversial questions in the large group. Moving from individual reflection to dyads or small groups before engaging in large-group dialogues can help individuals take progressively greater risks. The high priority given to exploring difficult issues, sharing vulnerabilities, and taking risks in intergroup dialogue makes it vital that a strong foundation be built early to encourage affective ties among participants. Participants are more likely to voice their thoughts and feelings openly and to take risks in an emotionally safe setting where they feel for and care about one another. Even though we acknowledge that no absolutely safe place exists in a society marked by social stratification, division, and hostilities, some removal from contentious debate, gaming, and advantage seeking is essential for meaningful dialogue to occur.

Given the societal constraints that discourage honest exploration and contemporary patterns of dominance and subordination and their effects on individuals, many participants will be reluctant to step outside their comfort zones to explore new territory without both support and challenge (the "push and pull" dynamics of learning encounters). We therefore rely on the group developmental stages of forming, storming, norming, working, and ending (Weber, 1982) to sequence the IGD group process and learning. For instance, in the formation stage of the group, participants may explore hopes and fears, generate group guidelines for engagement, begin to practice the habits of dialogue, and get to know each other. In the next stage (storming), participants may need to be challenged to question one another and prior knowledge and go beyond prior (often stereotypic) assumptions and accustomed ways of behaving and interacting. Mapping the causes and effects of group inequality can help clarify the relationship among the social identity groups in the dialogue. Once norms and relations are more established in the group, inquiring into controversial topics such as reverse discrimination, reproductive rights, and racial profiling helps to uncover the complex dynamics underlying interpersonal, community, and institutional relationships across the social identity groups participating in a dialogue.

The Four-Stage Design of Intergroup Dialogue

The educational design of intergroup dialogue relies on stages or phases of dialogue (Saunders, 1999; Stephan and Stephan, 2001; Zúñiga and Nagda, 2001) to map the topics and activities of the sequential design. The four stages, elaborated below, build on one another and sequence the movement in the intergroup dialogue from group beginnings to exploring differences and commonalities to dealing with hot topics or difficult questions to considering or taking action (see Exhibit 1). This design is a conceptual framework that allows facilitators and participants to understand the progression of goals, objectives, topics, and activities that support their work together.

Stage 1—Group Beginnings: Forming and Building Relationships

In the first stage, the focus is on establishing the foundation for creating an environment conducive to honest and meaningful exchange. The main goal of this stage is to support the formation of the dialogue group and build relationships across differences. Facilitators focus on creating a safe space for participants to share their thoughts and experiences. They begin to lay the groundwork for future sessions by attending to group building as well as introducing participants to the meaning of dialogue. Participants discuss why it is important to talk about the focus of the dialogues (see "Why Talk About Race/Ethnicity, Gender, or . . . ?" in the appendix) and their hopes and fears about the experience, identify needs and expectations, and establish guidelines for communication and confidentiality. Distinctions are drawn between dialogue and debate (Huang-Nissen, 1999; see "Dialogue and Debate" in the appendix), and the importance of speaking clearly from the mind and heart is emphasized. Participants are introduced to the characteristics of dialogue and subsequently practice some of the skills involved (see "Building Blocks of Dialogue" in the appendix). The activities in Stage 1 begin the process of building relationships and exploring personal and social identities. Two to three sessions are usually scheduled for this stage.

Stage 2—Exploring Differences and Commonalities of Experience

During the second stage, social identity–group commonalities and differences are explored. Although this stage is where the goal of consciousness raising is given primary focus, clarifying and sharing information about multiple social

EXHIBIT 1

Overview of the Four-Stage Design of Intergroup Dialogue

Stage	Content and Process Objectives		Structured Activities and Dialogue Starters
	Content Objectives	*Process Objectives*	
STAGE 1 Group Beginnings: Forming and Building Relationships (2–3 sessions)	• Build knowledge, values, and skills for dialogue • Clarify the meaning of "dialogue" and other forms of communication	• Establish the foundations for honest and meaningful dialogue	• Engaging in group-building activities; exploring goals and expectations • Distinguishing dialogue from debate; introducing Bohm's four building blocks of dialogue (1990) • Practicing interactive communication: speaking, listening, paraphrasing, and giving and receiving feedback (Bidol, 1986) • Exploring personal and social identities
STAGE 2 Exploring Differences and Commonalities of Experience (3–4 sessions)	• Explore meaning of key terms such as prejudice, discrimination, and oppression and their impact on students' lived experiences • Increase awareness of multiple social group memberships and dynamics of inequalities • Promote understanding of the systemic basis of group differences and conflicts in perceptions and experiences	• Encourage listening and perspective taking of experiences and perceptions different from one's own • Explore meaning of key terms such as prejudice, discrimination, and oppression in personal experiences	• Exploring multiple social identities: cultural chest activity • Terminology activity to generate meaning about key terms • Discussion of Harro's cycle of socialization (2000b) • Identity-based discussions and fishbowls to encourage introspection and deeper dialogue: web of oppression activity

(Continued)

EXHIBIT 1
Overview of the Four-Stage Design of Intergroup Dialogue (Continued)

Stage	Content and Process Objectives		Structured Activities and Dialogue Starters
	Content Objectives	Process Objectives	
STAGE 3 Exploring and Discussing Hot Topics (3–5 sessions)	• Explore differences and similarities of perceptions/experiences of controversial issues across and in social identity groups • Encourage analysis of systems of privilege, power, and oppression • Explore some of the roots of conflicting perceptions and experiences (historical, cultural, institutional, interpersonal)	• Encourage informed/ meaningful dialogue and inquiry • Probe for deeper levels of thinking, feeling, and responding	• Dialogues about controversial topics • Hot topics vary, depending on IGD focus. They may include interracial relationships, reproductive rights, safety on campus, separation and self-segregation on campus, sexuality and religion, gender and the media, immigration, affirmative action, marriage and civil unions. • Use a dialogue starter to ground and open the conversation such as movie clips, a gallery walk, or a take-a-stand activity followed by extensive debriefing, questioning, and dialogue.
STAGE 4 Action Planning and Alliance Building (2–3 sessions)	• Explore range of continuing learning opportunities and actions to promote diversity and social justice • Explore ways of moving from dialogue to action	• Bring closure to the dialogue experience	• Discussion of Harro's cycle of liberation (2000a) • Develop action plans and skits to illustrate various ways of taking action for inclusion and social justice • Affirmation activities to bring dialogue experience to a close

identities requires the development of mutual trust and provides another way to build trust and relationships among group members. Moreover, consciousness raising requires understanding how those identities reflect systems of social power and resource allocation and are often expressed in conflictual relations among groups. In this stage, members of both privileged and disadvantaged groups begin to understand their roles in maintaining systems of social discrimination and oppression through structured activities such as the web of oppression (see appendix), readings, and reflective writing. They can also explore both the views and interests they hold in common and those in which they differ or conflict.

These issues of dominance and subordination are often played out in the actual conduct of the dialogue. Because participants coming from different identities and backgrounds bring with them varying amounts of social power, generally reflecting their status positions in the society, some participants may talk more often, dominate air time, and overinfluence the direction of discussion. Other students may talk less, participate less actively in group activities, or withdraw from engagement. To overcome these typical patterns, it is necessary to foster the development of a relatively safe place where participants can take risks in sharing and inquiring into each other's perspectives and experiences even if it means asking "dumb" questions, departing from stifling norms, and entering potentially conflictual turf. Dialogic methods and structures that encourage speaking and active listening in dyads, triads, affinity groups, and fishbowls are widely used in this stage (see the appendix). Three to four sessions are usually scheduled for this stage.

Stage 3—Exploring and Dialoguing About Hot Topics

The third stage of intergroup dialogue involves dialogue about controversial topics or hot-button issues that cause tension between people of different social identity groups. The topics selected for discussion vary according to the focus of the intergroup dialogue. For example, in a dialogue about race and ethnicity, students or facilitators may select topics such as interracial dating, separation and self-segregation on campus, racial profiling, immigration, affirmative action, and racism on campus. In a gender dialogue, such topics might include single-sex or coed residence halls, friendship between men and women, safety

---

Intergroup Dialogue in Higher Education   29

on campus, reproductive rights, gender and the media, and sexism on campus. In a dialogue focusing on gender and sexuality, topics might include families and relationships, gender roles, compulsory heterosexuality, sexuality and religion, marriage and civil unions, and campus policies regarding benefits for partners and gender-neutral bathrooms.

Participants are encouraged to identify and voice their perspectives on and experiences with such issues and then to relate their position on an issue to the members of their social group. At the same time, participants are discouraged from stressing the rightness or wrongness of any position and encouraged to engage in dialogue, not debate. The ability to explore difficult topics in a trusting environment depends on a continued emphasis on consciousness raising and relationship building. It also calls for both support and challenge for risk taking. The intentional use of various structured activities and dialogue methods can support a range of participation styles and modes of questioning, listening, and responding to deepen the conversation (see "Getting Conversations Started" and "Methods for Deepening the Conversation" in the appendix). Activities such as dialogue about the dialogue can be helpful in identifying which aspects of the dialogue process are going well and not so well for participants. The third stage typically schedules one session per hot topic and includes one open session during which participants may explore emergent topics or issues or hold a question-and-answer session. Three to four sessions are usually scheduled for this stage.

Stage 4—Action Planning and Alliance Building

The final stage of intergroup dialogue builds on the prior stages but also shifts the discussion from reflection and dialogue to taking individual and group actions with others. As participants understand more about the personal and social costs of systems of discrimination and privilege and their own enmeshment in these systems, many are moved to think about taking action and engaging in efforts at social change. Some of these action plans or commitments may focus on individual behaviors such as one's own discriminatory behavior or prejudiced statements by roommates or parents, while others may focus on institutional policies and programs such as biased admissions policies or evidence of racism and sexism on campus. Because many of these activities may be undertaken in concert with others—or at least with the support and advice of others—attention is paid to building alliances and developing collaboration in and across social identity groups. In this last stage, participants also acknowledge everyone's contribution to the dialogue process and celebrate the collective effort. Two sessions are usually scheduled for this stage.

The four-stage design is not a rigid formula, and it is pedagogically important that the educational design match the flow of participants' organic learning processes. Although the stages may appear to be linear in their progression, intergroup dialogues may flow back and forth between stages as participants address and work through relationships and issues in the dialogue. Practitioners using the design may also need to adjust the topics covered in each stage to match specific group dynamics or participants' needs. For instance, intergroup dialogues launched in volatile environments may need to consider participants' emotional needs carefully and perhaps rely on much preparatory work to set the stage for dialogue (see, for example, Saunders, 1999, for methods used in high-conflict situations).

Practice Principles for Intergroup Dialogue

Although the four-stage educational design model provides a blueprint for the IGD curriculum, several underlying principles inform the planning and facilitation of the intergroup dialogue. Instead of an either/or approach, these principles focus on integrating person and structure, exploring commonalities and differences, and linking reflection and action. All practice principles integrate content and process concerns.

Integrating Person and Structure

In intergroup dialogue, attention must be given to both the personal and structural aspects of social group distinctions. The intergroup focus of intergroup dialogue requires that participants develop an understanding of the group-based nature of differences among people and the ways in which individuals are located in and experience systems of group privilege or subordination. Intergroup dialogue also addresses interpersonal and intergroup experience and analysis. By integrating and balancing these perspectives, intergroup dialogue invites participants to consider various manifestations and explanations of group differences. This aspect is important because of the tendency to explain the causes and effects of racism and other forms of oppression by focusing on the motivations and actions of individual people. Group and structural perspectives are necessary in a society that encourages us to think that the "social world begins and ends with individuals" (Johnson, 2001, p. 84). Although it is important to hold individuals accountable for biased and discriminatory actions, the prevalence of individualistic thinking can distort understanding of social events by underscoring the notion that an individual's values, attitudes, behaviors, and ideologies can be understood apart from social norms and structures. Furthermore, Johnson (2001) argues, individualistic thinking can paralyze conversations between people from privileged and targeted groups because it conveys the message that racial and gender oppression are, for example, a person of color's problem or a woman's problem rather than everyone's problem. At the same time, it is important to avoid the suggestion that macrosocietal and historical forces so overdetermine daily life that no personal responsibility or choice exists for individuals of more- or less-privileged groups. Considerations of personal agency and the relevance of both personal and structural levels of analysis can help to counter the passivity and inertia that often result from this tendency.

As mentioned earlier, conceptual organizers such as Harro's cycle of socialization (2000b) can be valuable in helping frame conversations that address both personal and structural dimensions of social identity. When combined with testimonial narratives focusing on a diverse range of socialization experiences, these activities help participants to reflect on their own and others' experiences growing up as members of more- or less-privileged groups. The idea that group differences are socially constructed and both emanate from and lead to social stratification may help participants from different groups understand why some of their experiences have been so different. Subsequent content may examine the ways that these differences have been organized institutionally, culturally, and personally to establish and maintain patterns of societal oppression and privilege.

Person-structure integration may also occur when participants are encouraged to consider how social institutions such as the economic system, legal system, educational system, and organized religion shape and regulate the attitudes and behaviors of members of advantaged and disadvantaged social groups. Breaking away from individualistic thinking starts when participants in the dialogue begin to realize that they are all implicated and affected in one way or another by the patterns of inclusion and exclusion reflected in the operation of these systems (Hardiman and Jackson, 1992; Johnson, 2001). Structured activities such as the web of oppression can visually illustrate the systematic nature of prejudice, discrimination, and oppression and the roles we all play in reinforcing power and privilege (see "Web of Oppression" in the appendix). Readings, fact sheets, cultural artifacts, and conceptual organizers such as Katz's levels and types of oppression (1978) can further help participants to understand and integrate the personal and structural dimensions of power, privilege, and exclusion in educational, legal, and economic systems.

Exploring Commonalities and Differences

Intergroup dialogue strives to find a balance between exploring differences and finding common ground. Doing so can be difficult in a pluralistic society where both difference and sameness are often emotionally loaded because of the ways that these categories have been used or are commonly understood. The emphasis may be placed on the values and interests that people have in common to promote social cohesion, on the one hand, or to render invisible real differences in status, opportunity, and power, on the other. Similarly, targeted or disadvantaged groups may emphasize group differences to resist cultural assimilation or build solidarity in their group, while this same emphasis, taken to an extreme, may prevent recognition of shared interests or the development of cross-group coalitions. Intergroup dialogue assumes that it is equally important to explore the issues, values, identities, experiences, and concerns that participants hold in common as well as those that differentiate them.

Many diversity education efforts in higher education aim for students to develop a sociohistorical understanding of inequalities and an increased awareness of culturally and institutionally supported prejudice and discrimination. Although necessary, Pharr (1996) argues, these educational goals are not sufficient if we are to truly engage across differences. We also need to grapple with each other's similar and distinct perspectives and to empathize with both joys and struggles with the hope of redefining and sharing power (Collins, 1993; Harro, 2000a; Pharr, 1996). Intergroup dialogues bridge the critical awareness dimensions that attend to how participants are differentially affected by systems of power and privilege through dialogic processes that are sustained over time. This form of communication facilitates the appreciation of different perspectives and the development of affective ties (Nagda, 2006). We discourage debates about pros and cons and discussions about right and wrong because they promote polarized interactions, usually at the expense of one of the sides of the argument (Huang-Nissen, 1999).

Commonalities and differences are often explored by situating participants' experiences in the context of their social identities as men, women, white people, people of color, or as appropriate for the particular dialogue group. In initial explorations of social identities, for instance, we introduce Harro's cycle of socialization (2000b), which maps the interpersonal, cultural, and institutional reinforcements of socialization on individuals based on their social group memberships. Participants then meet in social identity–based affinity groups (Zúñiga and Nagda, 1993b), where they explore thoughts, feelings, and experiences related to their racial, ethnic, gender, or other socialization, their lives on campus, and their interactions with members of the other group(s) in dialogue. When alone with members of their own group, targeted or disadvantaged group members often reveal the common and different ways in which they have experienced discrimination. At times, members who have had common experiences discover that only some have understood these experiences as a result of societal discrimination. At other times, they find that they have had different experiences resulting from intragroup differences based on gender, socioeconomic class, citizenship status, first language, religion, or sexual orientation. Similarly, members of dominant groups sometimes find that they can express perspectives and experiences associated with their privileged location more openly in their affinity group. They too may find that experiences that they thought were unique to them are actually more common with other members of their own group. At the same time, they learn that some of their experiences have been very different as a result of other social identities or experiences.

After meeting in their affinity groups, participants usually engage in a "fishbowl" activity to move the personal sharing to the large group. The purpose of a fishbowl is to support voicing and deep listening across the social identity groups participating in an intergroup dialogue. One group, seated in an inner circle with members of their own affinity group, dialogues about their insights from the separate group meeting. The other group, seated in an outer circle, listens to the dialogue but does not respond immediately. At the end of the first group's sharing, each member in the outer group may acknowledge one thing that he or she heard in listening to the inner group. This format is then repeated with the groups' switching roles (see the appendix). Following the structured fishbowl, participants are able to ask each other additional questions, bring in insights from readings and conceptual frameworks, and explore ways to deepen the dialogue as well as continue their own learning. In this way, participants begin to understand that their social identity–group experiences may be marked by similarities and differences across and in groups. Furthermore, participants are encouraged at this point to remember that personal experiences are influenced by historical, political, economic, social, and cultural dynamics.

In exploring differences and common ground, participants may also begin to see points of connection that develop out of a discussion about real or perceived differences. For example, participants in a gender dialogue who have listened empathically to women describing their fear and lack of safety walking on campus at night might learn that gay men, transgender individuals, men of color, people with physical disabilities, and others have also felt unsafe on campus. Facilitators may invite participants to identify how and why people feel unsafe and how such experiences might be similar and different for different groups. The next step in a gender dialogue might be for participants to discuss how working together to develop strategies for increasing women's safety on campus might be used to make the campus a safer place for everyone.

Linking Reflection and Action

Although many multicultural education efforts focus on increasing knowledge or awareness about discrimination and oppression, intergroup dialogue assumes that it is important for students to acquire knowledge and awareness *and* the skills and dispositions needed to become active participants in creating a more inclusive and socially just society. This acquisition is important because a major challenge faced by college students who want to translate their learning into concrete actions is knowing where to begin (Zúñiga, 2000). Like Tatum (1992), we believe it is unethical to ask students to critically examine issues of social oppression without offering hope and practical tools for creating change.

Through active, experiential, and dialogic methods, intergroup dialogue fosters critical reflection and strengthens individual and collective capacities to work in and across groups to promote social justice. This approach to learning fosters a dynamic and multidimensional (intrapersonal, interpersonal, intragroup, and intergroup) reflection process by which "an experience, in the form of thought, feeling or action, is brought to consideration" (Brockbank and McGill, 2000, p. 56). In intergroup dialogue, the issues brought forth may relate to participants' past experiences or they may involve here-and-now events that occur in the group's life (Marshak and Katz, 1999). Reflecting about these experiences may occur privately (through writing) or publicly in dyads or in the large group. Such exploration, however, involves more than just "sharing" and "getting to know you/getting to know myself" types of processes. These experiences are continually linked to reading that illuminates and analyzes the larger social, economic, cultural, and historical forces that shape people's perceptions and lives in different ways for different "kinds" of people.

The four-stage design provides a number of opportunities for participants to move from reflection to action. For instance, skill building, debriefing, and dialoguing support the development of dispositions and behaviors needed to engage in active and inquiry-focused learning about themselves and others (see "Methods for Deepening the Conversation" in the appendix). In addition, the design allows participants to understand enough about the dialogue process itself so that they can transfer their learning to other situations and endeavors. The opportunity to discuss the quality of interaction and discourse at the end of a session can transform conflicting relationships as participants gain a deeper understanding of why there is tension and misunderstanding and how to work with each other's realities. The ability to deal constructively with issues of conflict and injustice in the dialogue may then be applied to situations outside the dialogue.

Although an increased awareness of the causes and effects of group inequality is necessary for participants to improve relationships across differences or challenge social inequities, it does not necessarily lead to action for change outside the dialogue group (Chesler, 2001). Experimenting and practicing with new behaviors inside and outside the dialogue can actively support participants in developing new skills and commitments. As members of a small group that is also a microcosm of the larger society, IGD participants experience some of the issues that arise in groups (for example, inclusion-exclusion dynamics of norms guiding group engagement, membership, participation, and influence) and may replicate familiar intergroup power relations. Paying attention to and trying to change these processes in the group provides additional insights about ways participants can interrupt and change their own and others' behaviors that intentionally or unintentionally perpetuate oppressive group dynamics.

Even though the process of envisioning new commitments toward action for social justice is ongoing through the four stages of intergroup dialogue, it is most prominent in the third and fourth stages. Toward the end of Stage 2 or at the beginning of Stage 3, participants are encouraged to experiment with new behaviors. They are invited to deepen their conversations, to consider ways of applying what they have learned in their spheres of influence outside the dialogue, and, in some cases, to participate in action projects (see "Stage 4" in the appendix). They are encouraged to plan ways they can use their new individual and group skills to take collaborative actions that promote inclusion and social justice. Such carryover requires that participants clearly understand the process as well as the content lessons embodied in intergroup dialogue. When learning that occurs in an intergroup dialogue can be identified and named, it is more likely that participants will extend or translate these lessons to situations outside the dialogue.

To help participants develop confidence in taking action, skill-building activities, learning assignments, and role plays are incorporated in the design. For example, participants are invited to examine the action continuum (see the appendix) and their spheres of influence (self, friends, family, school, work, community) and to identify actions they might undertake in each sphere to intervene in unjust or hostile situations (Goodman and Schapiro, 1997). They can also prioritize actions and identify possible strategies and risks. This exercise moves the learning process from awareness and reflection to visualizing actual steps they can take to effect change. If time allows, role-play scenarios can also be enacted in which participants can practice taking action. Some participants will be more ready and committed than others to take action for social justice. Toward the end of the dialogue, some participants may be ready to change the world, while others may want to focus on learning more about social inequality and still others may be ready to alter their own personal attitudes and behaviors.

As is evident from this discussion, the three practice principles are themselves highly interrelated. Participants' ability to fruitfully explore commonalities and differences often relies greatly on understanding how societal structures affect their individual, personal experiences. Similarly, the bridging of differences can also positively affect their motivation and confidence to participate in social justice efforts. And as students engage more with the society at large, they discover more ways in which issues of inequality are manifest in their own educational institutions, the media, and in other aspects of their daily lives.

Facilitating Intergroup Dialogues

INTERGROUP DIALOGUE IS A *FACILITATED* LEARNING endeavor. This chapter discusses why facilitation is necessary, the competencies necessary for facilitation, how we prepare facilitators for their roles in dialogues, and the major challenges in facilitation. By facilitation, we mean active, responsive guidance, not formal instruction. Facilitators enable group members to develop their own processes and ways of gaining knowledge. Rather than simply presenting data, concepts, and theories, facilitators engage individual participants and the group in reflecting, sharing, and dialoguing about perspectives, feelings, and desires that are both personally intimate and socially relevant. Facilitators support and challenge participants to maximize their learning rather than evaluate individual participants on performance criteria. Facilitators are coparticipants, not experts; they learn as much, if not more, than participants in their group. Building on this brief definition of facilitation, the chapter discusses some of the principles of dialogue facilitation and the competencies required to perform this role. It then presents some examples of how IGD facilitators are trained for this work and concludes with some of the typical dilemmas and choices that facilitators confront in their work.

Why Facilitation and Cofacilitation?

The goals of intergroup dialogue—consciousness raising, building relationships across differences and conflicts, and strengthening individual and collective capacities to promote social justice—have strong implications for

---

group functioning and leadership. Three considerations are critical here. First, IGD's dialogic approach to education requires cofacilitators to avoid roles as "experts" but instead act as skilled and informed guides. Dialogic education also means that facilitators work to enrich and enhance participants' individual and group understandings of their lived experiences and social reality through a combination of structured activities, dialogic methods, readings, and conceptual information. Both in dialogue with their cofacilitator and other group members and in facilitating interactions among group members, facilitators model inclusiveness and fruitful engagement through listening, sharing, reflection, inquiry, and collaboration.

Second, a social justice approach to dialogue involves the facilitators in contextualizing individual and group processes in larger systems of oppression and privilege. Facilitators, as skilled group leaders, can help participants to work on these issues in ways that move them beyond their personal experience to a fuller appreciation of the role of oppressive social structures and hegemonic cultural norms in defining and affecting their lives. Facilitators rely on the design elements and practice principles discussed in the previous chapter to help guide the content and process of the dialogue sessions. When interaction in the group reflects larger sociopolitical processes (for example, men or other members of privileged social groups dominating the dialogue session or women or members of oppressed groups retreating into silence or erupting in anger), the facilitators need to illuminate it constructively. Or the facilitators may introduce concepts related to social inequality (such as prejudice, discrimination, privilege, and oppression) or controversial intergroup issues (such as safety on campus or affirmative action) into the group's dialogue. At the same time, facilitators can attend to how participants can move from reflection to action designed to interrupt discrimination and to promote inclusion and social justice.

For participants to engage in sustained and meaningful conversation that connects their own experiences about oppression and privilege to social structures and to responsibilities for engendering greater social justice, they must be both supported and challenged. Without sensitive guidance, the dialogue is likely to degenerate into overly cautious conversations or overly competitive and contentious debates and fights. The dialogic approach to working across differences calls for a partnership in facilitation—that is, cofacilitation—in which two facilitators reflect the identities of the social identity groups engaged in the dialogue. In this way, all participants have access to someone who has a social identity similar to their own, someone who has knowledge of their group's experiences, struggles, and hopes and who can empathize with the learning edges that come up in intensive cross-group engagement.

IGD facilitators are therefore *part* of the learning process and not *apart* from the group or the dialogues (Nagda, 2007). They are involved in their own development and learning while facilitating, and they practice an effective use of self to support and challenge the group's learning. Cofacilitators are not neutral or impartial but multipartial and balanced as a team in supporting all group members. Cofacilitators share power and control with each other and with members of the dialogue group in ways that make the best use of everyone's skills and abilities.

Competencies Required for Facilitators of Intergroup Dialogue

In the preparation and support of facilitators for intergroup dialogues, the emphasis is on skills for fostering the learning of others. Specific facilitation skills include cultivating opportunities for change in individuals and groups that foster the three goals of intergroup dialogue: consciousness raising, building relationships across differences and conflicts, and strengthening individual and collective capacities to promote social justice. Facilitators help participants to strategically analyze individual, intergroup, and group dynamics and to intervene appropriately to improve group functioning (see Exhibit A2 in the appendix). They collaboratively design, plan, and facilitate weekly sessions that attend to both the content of participants' learning and to individual and group processes. On most campuses, facilitators use curricula specific to their intergroup dialogues rather than planning from scratch, but they must be able to assess how the learning and dialogic process is unfolding in the group and the impact of the educational design on individuals and on the group, and then adjust the curricular design if necessary. Because facilitators work in pairs and in conjunction with participants in their group, they are called on to provide positive and constructive feedback directly and openly to one another and to ask for and receive feedback from group members.

A key facilitation task is to transform "critical incidents" into "teaching moments." For instance, inquiry into issues of personal identity or social attitudes and values (or hot topics) may occasionally so heighten participants' emotional vulnerability or sense of threat that they react dramatically—with defensiveness, aggression, anger, yelling, tearfulness, silence, or retreat. Such critical incidents may appear (or feel) dysfunctional to dialogue, but in fact they can be the opportunity for meaningful learning (Zúñiga and Chesler, 1993). Forthrightly addressing such incidents can help all participants learn more about each other and about the significant effects of difference, oppression, and privilege. Facilitators may aid the development of teachable moments by asking probing questions geared to both cognitive and affective learning, by modeling risk taking in intervening in these situations, and by addressing oppressive behaviors and dynamics in the group. Such actions allow dialogue participants to learn about and to improve the dynamics of inequality inside and outside the group as well as to allow others to hear about and alter their behavior.

Successful and effective facilitation requires integrating knowledge and awareness in a timely and intentional manner (also see Beale, Thompson, and Chesler, 2001; Nagda and others, 2001).

As to content, facilitators must have conceptual and empirical knowledge about the nature of prejudice, discrimination, and institutionalized privilege and oppression. They not only must know the definitions of these terms but also understand the current debates and struggles about their meaning and use (for example, prejudice, racism, aversive racism, color-blind racism, white racism, institutional racism, internalized racism, racial oppression). As to process, they must have similar facility with the differences among dialogue, discussion, debates, and fights and knowledge of group and intergroup dynamics (Ellinor and Gerard, 1998; Huang-Nissen, 1999).

As mentioned earlier, facilitators are very much a part of the IGD learning process even while they are facilitating others' learning. Thus, the *personal awareness* they bring to the dialogue needs to be effectively mobilized to serve as a resource. For instance, they must be in touch with and express their own awareness, empathy, and compassion for others and themselves to be effective. They must understand and be sensitive to the impact of their social identity–group memberships on themselves, their cofacilitation relationship on others in the group, and vice versa. And they must be in tune with their own learning process in the context of the group such that it does not take over participants' learning. Such private awareness and public demonstrations of skill and commitment can make the difference in the intensity, authenticity, and transformative nature of intergroup dialogue. As a result, facilitators and participants can better work through the challenges that necessarily arise over the duration of the dialogues.

Preparing Facilitators for Intergroup Dialogues

Providing competent facilitators for intergroup dialogues requires recruiting people who are ready to learn or use the knowledge, awareness, and skills required and preparing them for the particular dynamics of intergroup dialogues that differ from many other team or group discussions and settings. This section discusses the recruitment and screening of potential facilitators, the need for deliberate programs of training and support for them, examples of particularly useful formats or learning structures for facilitators' development, and the necessity of helping them form a supportive multicultural community as they proceed.

Recruiting and Screening Potential Facilitators

IGD programs have used different members of the college community as facilitators. A very few have used college or university faculty. Much more common is the participation of staff members from college and university student affairs offices. These professional colleagues—faculty and staff—often are drawn to IGD work by a commitment to student learning about personal and social matters, and they often have been trained in small-group facilitation skills. On a very few campuses, graduate or undergraduate students serve as peer facilitators of other graduate or undergraduate students in intergroup dialogue.

Some colleges and universities allow all interested potential facilitators—faculty, staff, and students—to participate in training as volunteers. Other colleges and universities with training targeted mostly to students have credit-based classes with open enrollment. Some schools require interested students to submit a written application and to participate in a series of individual and group interviews. On these bases, program staffs gather more useful and relevant information about these students ahead of time and can substantially upgrade the effectiveness of the selection process.

Criteria important in selecting facilitators center more on readiness for learning and engaging in a democratic, active learning process than on proved effectiveness to facilitate or teach; growth in the latter competencies can be developed through training programs. Previous experience as an IGD participant or participation in other experiential or social justice education efforts is always helpful. Although knowledge of intergroup issues is important, it also needs to be supported by having the potential to facilitate as a guide, colearner, and collaborator, not as an expert. Finally, it is important that facilitators as a group are diverse and mirror the range of social identities represented in actual dialogues. Such diversity enables them to build a multicultural community and to demonstrate the nature and value of such a model to dialogue participants.

Preparation and Ongoing Support for Facilitator Training

Experienced leaders of intergroup dialogue generally facilitate the training. (Some of the learning structures presented in this section are drawn directly from Beale, Thompson, and Chesler, 2001. Permission granted by the authors.) In most cases, two or more instructors are involved, representing different social identity groups (based on race or ethnicity, gender, class, and sexual orientation) and different statuses in the organizational hierarchy of the college or university (faculty member and student affairs staff member or graduate student). Once again, this staffing model mirrors the cofacilitation design of the intergroup dialogues themselves. One structure for training potential graduate and undergraduate student facilitators consists of a semester- or quarter-long course focusing on prefacilitation training and involving a mix of weekly sessions and often a two- or three-day overnight retreat. Many students remark on the importance of the retreat because it promotes intense and concentrated work and allows participants to bond. At the end of the training course, some learners are selected to facilitate intergroup dialogues. Not everybody is quite ready for this task, whether through their own preference or the instructor's decision. Those selected proceed to the support sessions accompanying their actual facilitation work. In some programs, the practicum is formalized and meets concurrently with the actual facilitation work to provide support, debriefing opportunities, and ongoing in-service training.

A variety of intellectual materials help participants to explore the history and cultural traditions of different social identity groups and the relevance of these traditions and experiences for resultant personal styles and behaviors. An explicit focus also must be directed to issues of domination and privilege, the appreciation of differences, structures, and cultures of oppression, and challenges to these patterns. The examination of interpersonal, intergroup, and societal conflict is an important ingredient of the training. Although differences and conflict are emphasized, a high priority must also be placed on understanding communal or transidentity group issues and the history and tactics involved in efforts to form coalitions or alliances across particular identity groupings. Exhibit 2 shows one training model.

Striking a balance between preparation in the substance of intergroup relations issues and in the skills of small-group instructional facilitation takes on prime consideration in term-long training structures. Learning about and practicing both these sets of competencies reflect the integration of content and process that parallels work on the issues that also come up in the intergroup dialogue. As such, the training group serves as a living learning laboratory.

Using Multidimensional Instructional and Learning Strategies. Given that intergroup dialogues themselves are complex in their cognitive, affective, and action dimensions of learning, we use multiple formats in training facilitators. Not only does this approach engage the learning styles and preferences of different facilitators and expand their learning styles, it also models for them the different learning structures used in the intergroup dialogue itself.

Structured experiential *activities* allow trainees to integrate cognitive and affective dimensions of learning about intergroup issues. Role plays (dialogue versus debate, for example), simulations (see *Starpower* by Shirts, 1977, for example), and collaborative problem-solving activities (see Bavelas, 1972; Johnson and Johnson, 2003) provide a common reference point for reflective and dialogic engagement of all participants. Debriefing such activities usually includes reflection on and examination of the formation and maintenance (or change) in social identities, dynamics of stratification and oppression, the transition to resistance and empowerment,

EXHIBIT 2
Intergroup Dialogue Facilitation Training Design

Creating the Learning Space	Diving Deep and Surfacing: Feeling, Thinking, and Doing Intergroup Dialogue	Practicing Intergroup Dialogue Facilitation
Setting the Stage • Provide an orientation to the course, the instructors, and IGD facilitation. • Get acquainted with each other and how we work in groups. • Reflect and share our passion for engaging in IGD work. • Assess strengths and areas of growth for IGD facilitation. • Articulate initial ground rules for establishing a learning community. ***Conceptual and Experiential Roots of Intergroup Dialogue*** • Engage in a dialogue about our hopes and fears.	***Weekend Retreat*** • Link Harro's cycle of socialization (2000b) and cycle of liberation (2000a) conceptual organizers to IGD work. • Understand social identity development models and their impact on dialogues. • Discuss communication dynamics between in groups and out groups. • Understand the connections between facilitation role, intergroup dynamics, and relations. • Observe and identify group facilitation skills and approaches throughout the retreat. • Engage in different alliance-building activities throughout the retreat. • Understand the nature of conflict (styles, strategies, and tactics) in groups and engage in analyses and problem solving of conflict scenarios.	• Understand the different aspects of facilitating educational designs. • Practice implementation of educational activities and group facilitation. • Observe facilitation/cofacilitation practice and provide positive and constructive feedback to fellow facilitators. • Continue generating improved and new educational activities to serve as resource for facilitators. ***Coming to a Close and Transitioning to Next Term*** • Wrap up IGD facilitation practice. • Reflect on our learning together in the facilitation course.

- Lay the foundations for IGD: (1) Freirean dialogic education (1970); (2) Bohm's four building blocks of dialogue (1990) and Bidol's interactive communication (1986); (3) active and experiential learning; (4) social justice approach to dialogue.
- Practice some skills for dialogue related to Bohm's building blocks of dialogue (1990).

Group Processes, Intergroup Dynamics, and Intergroup Dialogue Facilitation

- Introduce group dynamics, group development, and group observation.
- Discuss the connection between group stages and facilitation role.
- Identify pertinent facilitation skills at different stages of intergroup dialogue.

- Begin cofacilitator team building.
- Engage in problem-solving facilitation scenarios.
- Introduce design planning and prepare for practice for Sessions 5 to 7.

Postretreat Reconnecting

- Reflect and dialogue about retreat experiences and reentry.
- Make a transition to student-led facilitation practice.

- Make a transition to IGD facilitation in the next term.
- CELEBRATE!!

SOURCE: Developed by B. A. Nagda for the Intergroup Dialogue, Education, and Action Center, University of Washington School of Social Work.

and the development of strategies that can be used to address change effectively and achieve more equitable allocations of power and resources—both in the dialogue and in the organization or community at large.

Dialogic structures use a mix of large- and small-group learning formats. Large-group discussions are used in the beginning of the training to build a community of learners through establishing guidelines for participation, participating in trust-building and getting-acquainted activities, and engaging in some dialogue about the hopes and fears that facilitators bring to the facilitation. As the training progresses, large groups become critical for sharing information, discussing readings, debriefing and dialoguing about structured activities, and examining the intergroup issues and patterns developing among participants and groups in the training course. Large groups are also helpful in the collective exploration and processing of facilitation dynamics. Small-group discussions and activities are helpful in building trust and safety in the group. They promote more personal and intimate sharing about social identities and serve as an arena for organizing collective projects. Small-group structures also provide a context for participants to experience the processes and concepts of group dynamics, observe and reflect on these dynamics, and learn to think more intentionally about facilitation and intervention.

Minilectures, in the form of didactic presentations and conceptual organizers, orient trainees to the important theoretical and conceptual components of the learning. We refer to them as minilectures intentionally; they are not meant to be the sole or primary basis of learning but to serve as a stimulant for reflection and dialogue or as a way to synthesize the ongoing reflections and dialogues.

Building a Community Among Facilitators and Instructional Leaders. Part of the training focuses on individuals' separate social identities, principally to help trainees better understand themselves and their own social identity group. Another part focuses on helping trainees to understand the identities, cultures, social experiences, and outlooks of other groups. Both foci are part of IGD ideology and practice. Thus, a diverse group of potential facilitators is an absolutely essential component of any training program. It also is important for trainees to understand and appreciate one another and to bond as a community that cuts across separate identity groups' interests, ideologies, or social locations. Such a community provides the trust and safety necessary to support an intense learning experience. But it is important to develop such a community in a real, impassioned, and committed way, not in a way that paints over important differences and inevitable conflicts. These dynamics also surface in the actual intergroup dialogue, but it has a much more intense reality in the context of an intimate training program for group facilitators—especially on a weekend retreat. Several structures and processes help to build community.

Learning partners is a format that allows trainees to learn with and from each other during training. Partnership provides a forum for participants to debrief structured activities as well as to explore some of the knowledge and awareness dimensions of facilitation. Learning partners also explore their hot buttons related to social identity–based issues (issues that trigger their own personal passions) and blind spots (areas of which they are not aware or have a very limited awareness). Facilitators also draw on the partnering relationship to bounce ideas, gain and provide feedback, and potentially prepare to be cofacilitators.

Participating in some of the IGD activities used by the IGD educational design (see appendix), facilitated by training instructors, allows all participants to experience the dialogue process. Thus, if trainees have not been involved in an intergroup dialogue, they now get first-hand experience in what intergroup dialogue might be like.

Practicing facilitation is critical to developing the skills for facilitation and the confidence of facilitators in engaging in what for some may be a very novel experience. Practice facilitation can occur in different ways, both inside and outside the instructional space:

Minifacilitation of small-group dialogues in class to get familiar with the feel of facilitation;

Facilitating an intergroup dialogue with members of the facilitator's own social identity group outside class;

In-class cofacilitation of a structured activity or session from the IGD curriculum design and use of the skills they want to improve (see Exhibit A1 in the appendix);

Partnering with another trainee of a different social identity group, convening several members of both those identity groups, and cofacilitating a discussion of a hot topic outside class.

All these practice efforts also help future facilitators to explore, express, and test the reality of their personal hopes and fears about the role they are about to play.

Personal time allows participants to reflect on the training activities and to integrate the multidimensional learning in the training. Trainees are encouraged to write about their experiences in a journal, to share with a colleague or learning partner with whom they feel close, to draw on instructors as a resource, or simply to spend time alone. It is important to cast this time not as an alternative to the group experience but as a complement that can help to deepen the dialogues.

Sustaining Structures During Facilitation

Facilitating intergroup dialogues is part of life-long learning about social identity and intergroup issues that becomes more complex and is never complete. Given the normal pressures of collegiate and work life, the initial training experience starts to fade if not followed by continuing meetings and work throughout the term. Moreover, sometimes the reality of facilitating an intergroup dialogue does not hit until the facilitators are actually involved in such work; then the opportunity for growth and development is truly great. Thus, most programs have designed a term-long follow-up to the prefacilitation training program that continues to work with facilitators while they conduct dialogues. In addition, different coaching and facilitation debriefing methods engage facilitators in reflective learning processes to continue learning by doing.

Observation and Feedback. At some schools with well-established training sequences and resources, training instructors sit in on one or two dialogue sessions to observe the cofacilitation team and to provide feedback. Although strategizing ahead of time and debriefing are useful, actual observation provides new information for reflection and feedback.

Consultations. As part of feedback (with or without observation), many programs schedule individual meetings to allow training instructors to work closely with the cofacilitators and to talk about issues that are particular to the group or participants with whom they are working. Consultation or coaching can also assist in team building by exploring cofacilitation dynamics, working through differences, misunderstandings, or conflicts, and suggesting how facilitators can support each other.

Microfacilitation. As part of in-service training in some colleges and universities, cofacilitators videotape some of the sessions they facilitate to better assess how well they are working together facilitating the dialogue, working with group dynamics, and so on. They can meet on their own to watch the videotape or to identify a segment they would like to dissect and analyze in greater depth with their consultant.

Major Issues and Challenges in Facilitating Intergroup Dialogues and Programs

The growing literature on intergroup dialogues as well as our own experience with them help identify a series of common issues faced by program faculty and facilitators. These issues arise as a function of the features of intergroup dialogue, of the very characteristics that make it an attractive and exciting approach to intergroup learning. The issues are divided into two major categories: (1) recruiting and training facilitators (both faculty members and students) and (2) actually facilitating intergroup dialogues (dealing with the nature of the facilitator's and cofacilitator's roles, with facilitators' and participants' reactions to the innovative pedagogy involved, and connecting participants' social identities to group dynamics).

Issues in Recruiting and Training IGD Facilitators

Faculty Participation and Preparation. The involvement of faculty and undergraduate students in leadership roles in IGD activities represents distinct challenges for IGD programs.

We indicated earlier that it is relatively rare for tenured or tenure-track faculty members to be heavily involved in IGD programs. The relative absence of regular faculty members from this activity is probably a reflection of three factors: (1) the institutional and disciplinary barriers (including lack of rewards) for IGD facilitation; (2) the high level of energy, time, and involvement with students required by intergroup dialogue; and (3) the relative lack of skill in this pedagogical practice among traditionally trained faculty members. The first barrier can be addressed as IGD programs gain greater attention on college campuses and if innovative educators are successful in their efforts to broaden traditional and research-oriented faculty career lines. The power of the second and third barriers also may be ameliorated as faculty explore new pedagogies and recognize their students' desire for alternative instructional modes—in intergroup dialogue and elsewhere throughout the curriculum. Nevertheless, unless institutional priorities change dramatically, we expect that faculty involvement in intergroup dialogue will remain limited to a relatively small and highly committed cadre.

Students as Peer Facilitators. This approach represents a more learner-focused and democratic pedagogical structure than either staff or faculty facilitation. Peer facilitation suggests that students can learn outside the traditional patterns of faculty control and direction of the instructional process. Thus, it can make specific contributions to intergroup encounters and more broadly to the empowerment of learners, both in intergroup dialogue and in other areas of higher education. In the particularly intensive and challenging context of intergroup dialogue, it may be easier for participants to share their confusions and hesitant inquiries and learning with a peer instructional leader than with more traditional, higher-status, and often older faculty and staff members. Entrusting the educational leadership of their peers to trained students involves a pedagogical challenge quite different from what students and faculty experience in their everyday campus lives, however.

Using trained undergraduate or graduate students as peer facilitators in intergroup dialogue entails some distinct risks:

Despite training, they often lack a substantive knowledge base in the social sciences, especially around issues related to prejudice, discrimination, privilege, and oppression.

They often lack skills in small-group leadership and instructional guidance.

Their authority and credibility may be challenged by their peers.

As a result of these factors, they often experience fear and anxiety about carrying out their new and unaccustomed roles, which is in itself disabling.

In addition, peer facilitators and peer-facilitated intergroup dialogue must deal with the press of traditional institutional forces that may look askance at undergraduate students' having any responsibility for instructional leadership of their peers (even though in most cases they explicitly do not have responsibility for grading their peers' work) and may not see intergroup dialogue itself as a viable academic experience. The press of these factors may be ameliorated by a well-thought-through training, supervision, and support program, especially one that helps facilitators to negotiate between their own learning needs and those of the participants with whom they work.

Issues in Facilitating Intergroup Dialogues

Intergroup dialogue's distinctive features provide a powerful learning opportunity for participants and facilitators. At the same time, these features carry with them particular issues and challenges that program staff must acknowledge, develop, and rectify.

The facilitator's authority and role are conceptualized differently in various programs. Two critical dimensions are important to consider: educator versus colearner and neutral versus partisan participant. Some IGD scholars and practitioners suggest that facilitators really are and should be seen as educators, while others emphasize the colearning dynamic present when everyone is committed to a learning process, regardless of their relative knowledge or skills. And some suggest that facilitators always are or should be neutral in delivering substantive material or helping participants to negotiate conflicts and difficult issues, while others suggest that facilitators must always be seeking to create more socially just conceptualizations, ways of relating with others, and ways of working in the world inside and outside the intergroup dialogue. Our own approach has been to support facilitators in the effective use of self in the group such that their own participation enhances rather than detracts from group learning.

Adopting and practicing a new and complex pedagogical process involves facilitators' sharing with participants the nature of intergroup dialogue and the experiential learning process at its heart. It is a colearning experience, with facilitators learning about themselves at the same time they seek to enhance participants' learning. One result is that facilitators as well as participants constantly are working on the edges of their own understanding to expand their knowledge, awareness, and skills. Although many IGD programs and many facilitators approach the task with some sort of predetermined script or syllabus, they must also be able to respond at the moment, in the moment, and organically to issues that inevitably arise.

It is particularly important for facilitators to be on the alert to move participants and the entire group beyond surface and trite conversation by asking questions, probing deeper, and expanding the conversation to include more members of the group. Additionally, probing may occur around intellectual or knowledge-based issues and assertions, but it is certainly needed when emotional issues surface or fail to surface. Skill is involved in knowing how to enter into and follow up on conversations to ask and probe more deeply. Courage also is required. Facilitators are naturally concerned about making mistakes, but the willingness to make mistakes and to ask and probe more deeply in the interest of true intergroup dialogue is at the heart of the entire endeavor. If facilitators are not prepared for and able to take such risks, participants certainly cannot be expected to do so.

In addition to learning an alternative pedagogy, facilitators need to deal with dialogue participants who also are new to this approach and who may expect an intergroup dialogue to use traditional forms of instruction and to involve an easy workload. Under such circumstances, participants may be surprised, perhaps resentful or alienated, by the pedagogical approach and the amount of reading and reflective writing inherent in credit-bearing intergroup dialogues. They may also question or challenge the authority, credibility, and credentials of the facilitator, especially a peer facilitator.

Relating with students and their expectations, facilitators also find themselves dealing with participants involved in all the typical dynamics one can expect in a small group. These generic group dynamics take a somewhat different shape in the context of intergroup dialogue as the power and sense of entitlement or disadvantage and exclusion associated with different participants' social identities come into play. Such social locations play out in intergroup dialogues through behavior that takes the form of dominant or subordinate participation in the group, long monologues, or extended silence. One facilitator expressed a commonly felt frustration at not knowing how to deal with a participant who was dominating the discussion: "I was getting frustrated with A's long soliloquies, but I didn't know how to ask him to back off or be quiet" (quoted in Beale, Thompson, and Chesler, 2001, p. 236).

Dealing with oneself and one's social identity involves facilitators' (or cofacilitators') being aware and knowledgeable about their own multiple social identities and being able to rely on their own personal journey into increased awareness. Just as IGD participants come to these encounters with misinformation and perhaps prejudices about members of other groups, they often target the facilitator as a source of inquiry or challenge about the meaning of her or his social identity and its relationship with others. Such inquiry or challenge may come from members of their own social identity groups as well as from others. Moreover, all such interaction may create situations in which facilitators are personally affected by issues connected to their salient social identities. Awareness and skill in working with such triggers can not only enhance facilitators' development but also contribute to a richer group experience (Bell, Washington, Weinstein, and Love, 1997).

Working effectively with different groups of participants involves working with participants from diverse groups who may, in turn, have different levels of sophistication, learning styles, trust in the process, or interest in the content of the intergroup dialogue. Bringing the group together to generate some common expectations and to pursue some common goals involves working with different hopes, fears, expectations, and needs and helping participants understand why they may differ. In a similar fashion, some typical small-group dynamics may take a different shape in an intergroup dialogue (see Exhibit A2 in the appendix). As one example, facilitators must deal with power and influence differentials among individual participants and with power issues associated with the social identities of participants in the intergroup dialogue. One woman facilitator expressed a concern that "the discussion was one-sided, with all the men talking. The men weren't dominating a discussion with the women but more just dominating the dialogue. We should have broadened it up more" (quoted in Beale, Thompson, and Chesler, 2001, p. 236). In terms of social identity, facilitators need to consider what intervention this facilitator or set of cofacilitators might have made, whether the woman or man facilitator should have made it, what different options the woman or man facilitator might have had at his or her disposal, and what the differential effect by the woman or man facilitator might have had on this participant and the group.

Working with conflict productively involves facilitators' dealing with participants who resist the process or are being defensive about certain topics of discussion. Much of this resistance is an expression of the desire to avoid conflict. But overt or covert intergroup conflict is what justifies and leads to the development of and participation in intergroup dialogue; as such, it cannot be avoided. Covert dynamics of this sort must be brought into the open. In addition to knowing how and when to surface covert conflict, facilitators must be able to respond when participants engage in heated conflict across or in identity groups.

Cofacilitation is not always easy. Dilemmas range from not fully understanding what a cofacilitator is communicating in the group to not following the same agenda or means of accomplishing the goals of the session to using different intervention strategies. According to one cofacilitator, "It would have been good here to ask [the participant] 'why does he think that?' However, [my cofacilitator] asked another question to get others involved. I wanted to say, 'Could we hold on to that question and ask this question [of the participant who just spoke]?' The reason why I felt that I shouldn't do that is because it makes us look unorganized" (quoted in Beale, Thompson, and Chesler, 2001, p. 236). These dilemmas might occur in any form of group setting—work groups, self-growth groups, or education groups. In intergroup dialogues, however, these issues can be magnified because the cofacilitators are intentionally from different racial or ethnic, gender, class, or sexual orientation groups; issues of power and culture add to the normal problems of interpersonal communication and interaction. In the absence of good preparation and debriefing, facilitators will be stuck with these sorts of dilemmas.

Finally, linking reflection and action remains a constant struggle for both program staff and facilitators. Although the final stage in the dialogue does focus on strengthening individual and collective capacities to promote social justice, some groups may not get to that stage for a variety of reasons. For example, in groups where there is no clear understanding or acknowledgment of structural inequality with personal consequences, many participants may feel that the issues do not apply to them. In other groups, controversy built up through the first three stages may require facilitators to engage the group in "healing" and relationship building before the end of the dialogues.

At other times, however, participants demand to know what they can do about the situation after being confronted with the enormity of structural inequalities and experiencing feelings such as guilt, sadness, anger, or helplessness. Facilitators may respond by saying that it is important for the dialogue process to unfold fully because the group will, in the final stage of the dialogues, talk specifically about taking actions toward personal and social change. Or they may actually start strategizing for action to retain participants' interest. These challenges all involve balancing reflection, dialogue, and action, integrating different forms of action throughout the dialogue, and reminding participants to recognize the many ways they are indeed involved in taking action. For the intergroup dialogue to lead to alliance building, facilitators need to engage the group in dialogue about their actions with a view of how those actions serve to maintain privilege and disadvantage or to challenge power imbalances.

Facilitating intergroup dialogues is a complex endeavor that calls for a holistic and skillful application of the knowledge, awareness, and values related to supporting the development of social identity, fostering relationship building across differences, and linking dialogue to action. Like participants, the most effective facilitators are those who approach intergroup dialogues with a learning orientation that is not only individual and self-focused but also collective and other-focused. Because intergroup dialogue relies heavily on the active involvement of all participants, facilitators must ensure that their learning agenda does not compromise participants' learning. At the program level, IGD coordinators must pay careful attention to the preparation and support of facilitators—from the initial training to actual facilitation to reflective learning-by-doing throughout the whole process.

Research on Outcomes and Processes of Intergroup Dialogue

THIS CHAPTER REVIEWS THE RESEARCH ON INTERGROUP dialogue in higher education. Because intergroup dialogue is a relatively new educational approach, the associated research is also new and evolving. In *Improving Intergroup Relations,* Stephan and Stephan (2001) emphasize that knowledge of research and evaluation results—whether positive or negative—is critical in advancing intergroup relations; it is important to know both what works and what does not work to refine programs. Two broad questions are addressed in this review: What do students gain by participating in intergroup dialogue? How do the educational design features and teaching-learning practices of intergroup dialogue influence the outcomes?

National, institutional, and classroom studies using various research methods show clearly that college students' engagement in intergroup dialogue has a significant and positive effect on their preparation for democratic participation (Gurin, Dey, Hurtado, and Gurin, 2002). The educational benefits of active engagement with diversity—both learning about diversity and interacting with diverse others in the classroom and on campus—were the crux of the empirical evidence presented in support of the University of Michigan's affirmative action cases in the Supreme Court (*Gratz* v. *Bollinger,* 2003; *Grutter* v. *Bollinger,* 2003). Diverse educational settings marked by novelty, disequilibrium, and dissonance in information and experiences combined with opportunities for substantive reflection and meaningful dialogue with others

NOTE: *Biren (Ratnesh) A. Nagda took the lead and primary responsibility for conceptualizing and writing this chapter.*

can have significant positive impact on participants (Nagda, Gurin, and Johnson, 2005). Hurtado's review (2003) suggests "participation in intergroup dialogue has a focused impact, with the most significant effects on students' perspective-taking skills (or capacity to see the world from someone else's perspective), the development of a pluralistic orientation, and the belief that conflict enhances democracy" (p. 20).

A Conceptual Framework for Research on Intergroup Dialogue

In the research and evaluation of intergroup dialogue, cross-sectional survey research focusing on knowledge and awareness (or attitudes) is most common, with some studies that use pre/post and longitudinal designs and a few in-depth qualitative studies. Almost all published work relies on self-reports by participants, both of dialogue processes and outcomes. Such self-reports of changed intergroup attitudes may not always be stable in time and place and may sometimes be inconsistent with actual behavior. Nevertheless, what has been published or presented at professional conferences is both interesting and instructive, and it provides practitioners and scholars with directions for future work.

Based on the work of Nagda, Kim, and Truelove (2004) and Nagda (2006), Figure 1 provides a conceptual framework to situate the research and evaluation of intergroup dialogue. We introduce the framework with the rightmost column on outcomes, focusing on the first question: What do students gain, both short term and long term, by participating in intergroup dialogues? We then work left to answer the second question: How do the educational design features of intergroup dialogue influence the outcomes? We end with the program approach, the first column: What about the program approach influences the educational design and the outcomes?

Outcomes

At its heart, intergroup dialogue is designed to enhance students' capacities to work with differences and to participate effectively in diverse settings in colleges and universities and later in more multicultural organizations and communities. The research reflects this focus on learning outcomes or goals

FIGURE 1

A Conceptual Framework for Research on Intergroup Dialogue

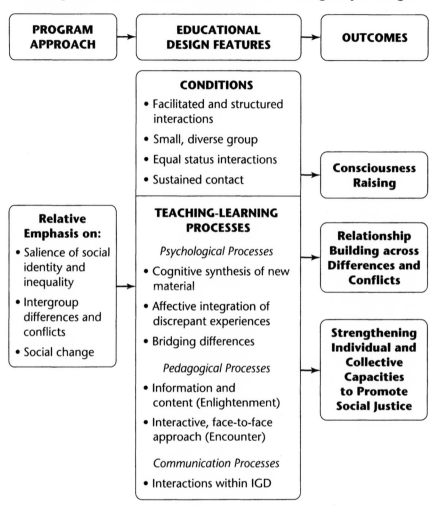

SOURCE: Developed by B. A. Nagda for the Multiversity Intergroup Dialogue Research Consortium.

discussed in earlier chapters—consciousness raising, building relationships, and strengthening individual and collective capacities for social change. Consciousness raising outcomes include, for example, awareness of one's and others' social identities and understanding structural inequality. Outcomes of relationship building include empathic perspective taking, communication across differences, and positive beliefs about the use of conflict. Outcomes of capacities for social change include commitment and confidence in prejudice reduction and promoting diversity and support for prodiversity institutional policies.

Although it clearly is important to know the outcomes of programs, it is also important to understand how the design features and teaching-learning processes in intergroup dialogue influence intended outcomes (the middle column in Figure 1) so as to improve specific program practices.

Educational Design

Educational design features include two components. First, conditions are aspects of the group and the learning encounter that help to structure intergroup dialogues and to influence the nature of intergroup contact and interaction (see "Design and Practice Principles in Intergroup Dialogue" earlier). Allport (1954), in prescribing the ideal ingredients for positive intergroup relationships among different groups, emphasized the conditions of equal status contact, interdependence, acquaintance potential, and authority sanction. In intergroup dialogues, they include factors such as the small-group setting, degree of equal status among participants, use of structured activities, and facilitation (Nagda, Balon, Hernandez-Morales, and Bouis, 2003; Nagda and Zúñiga, 2003; Werkmeister-Rozas, 2004).

Second, *teaching and learning processes* refers to a variety of different dimensions of psychological change, learning, and interactions that occur in the given conditions and influence the outcomes. Nagda (2006) conceptualizes them as psychological, pedagogical, and communication processes.

Psychological processes refers to the individual affective (for example, emotional empathy, comfort in communicating across differences) or cognitive (for example, assimilation of information about one's own group and the other group's histories and cultures) learning that happens in the intergroup dialogue. Although they are also outcomes in and of themselves, they are part of the learning processes in that they facilitate other outcomes (Dovidio and others, 2004; Nagda, 2006).

Pedagogical processes include the situational features of intergroup dialogue such as enlightenment or content-based, informational learning and encounter, or interactive learning (Dovidio and others, 2004; Lopez, Gurin, and Nagda, 1998). Khuri (2004), for example, found that students in an Arab-Jewish dialogue attributed most of their learning to hearing other students' views and to readings, the facilitator's comments, and video documentaries shown in class.

Communication processes, a distinctive theoretical contribution of intergroup dialogue to the field of intergroup contact, include the dialogic interactions in the intergroup dialogue (Nagda, 2006). Nagda and Zúñiga (2003), for example, found that the more students valued dialogic learning—sharing, colearning, inquiry, conflict exploration, and action planning—the more positive their learning outcomes, which may also be reflected in the quantity and quality of participation (Maoz, 2001; Maoz, Steinberg, Bar-On, and Fakhereldeen, 2002). For instance, storytelling and personal sharing in intimate interactions appear to foster comfort in interracial and interethnic situations, learning from diverse peers, reduction in unconscious prejudice, and capacity for leadership in a diverse democracy (Vasques-Scalera, 1999; Werkmeister-Rozas, 2004; Yeakley, 1998).

Program Approach

Program approach, the first column in Figure 1, refers to the particular theoretical or philosophical orientation of the program and is seen to guide the educational design, teaching-learning processes, and subsequent outcomes in intergroup dialogue. For example, Maoz (2004), discussing Palestinian-Jewish dialogues in Israel, distinguishes alternative approaches to dialogue in terms of a focus on coexistence (commonality/consensus building) or confrontation (difference/challenge). These different approaches to creating awareness, building relationships, and envisioning action may well lead to different outcomes for participants from different social locations. Intergroup dialogue, as conceived here, focuses on both commonalities and differences but emphasizes their contextualization in a larger sociopolitical reality. Thus, intergroup dialogue draws on aspects of both approaches currently identified in research literature. Unless otherwise noted, the research cited in this chapter refers specifically to research on the IGD model.

The conceptual framework helps to situate a number of studies highlighted below for their particular contributions to our understanding of intergroup dialogues. The studies included are neither exhaustive in detail nor inclusive of all relevant studies. Both large and small, quantitative and qualitative, published and unpublished studies are included to show the variety of ways to assess and learn about the impact of intergroup dialogue.

Outcomes of Intergroup Dialogue

At the University of Michigan, a quasi-experimental design using a pretest-posttest design was conducted to look at the impact of intergroup dialogue. First-year students enrolled in an introductory course that met the diversity requirement, "Intergroup Relations and Conflict," with intergroup dialogue as a major course component, were matched on race or ethnicity and gender with students who did not take the course. The matched sample was drawn from a concurrent institutional study investigating the diversity experiences of all entering first-year students. All the students were surveyed on entry to college and again at the end of their fourth year. Lopez, Gurin, and Nagda (1998) found that students in this course thought more structurally about racial and ethnic inequalities than did their counterparts. Furthermore, when presented with intergroup conflict scenarios, the same students endorsed more structural actions (such as changing the climate of the university and societal change) as responses to the situation than did their counterparts who were not in the course.

In another classroom-based study, one without a matched control group, a required introductory course in cultural diversity and social justice at the University of Washington expanded the scope of outcomes beyond consciousness raising. Students participated in weekly intergroup dialogues to complement the weekly didactic lecture sessions. Nagda, Kim, Moise-Swanson, and Kim (2006) show significantly increased outcomes in the areas of raising consciousness, bridging differences, and building capacity for social change. These findings held when results for students of color and white students were looked at separately, with one exception: students of color showed a significant increase in cognitive empathy, that is, perspective-taking ability, as a result of intergroup dialogue, but the same was not true for white students.

Zúñiga (2004), in an exploratory classroom study, grappled with a common concern in intergroup dialogue and related efforts: the link between dialogue and action. Undergraduate students in race or ethnicity and gender dialogues at the University of Massachusetts Amherst reported actions that they took or intended to take as a result of their participation. In the course, students participated in an intergroup collaboration action project in diverse teams of four to five students each. Using grounded theory (Strauss and Corbin, 1990), Zúñiga analyzed thirty-six students' final reflection papers and eight team action project reports. She identified three patterns. First, students defined action varyingly as taking risks, talking with others, and educating self and others. In other words, students' ideas of action taking mirrored the kind of actions they were learning to adopt in the dialogue. Second, students in the race or ethnicity dialogues drafted more elaborate plans for next steps than students in the gender dialogue. Students in the gender dialogue, however, appeared to be more engaged in applying what they were learning in the dialogue to conversations with their peers outside class. Third, women expressed a stronger desire to reach out and talk to people, while men seemed more inclined to apply what they had learned in a job or to take the message to the streets or to an organization to which they belonged. Thus, both the type of dialogue and the gender of participants influenced the kinds of actions students intended to take in the future.

These outcome studies show that intergroup dialogues are effective and that effectiveness is evidenced in students' greater intergroup understanding, increased motivation and skills for engaging across differences, and strengthened confidence in intergroup collaborations and in taking action toward greater social justice. These outcomes affirm IGD efforts. Yet we need to know more about how and what about intergroup dialogue helps foster these outcomes.

Conditions of Intergroup Dialogue

Werkmeister-Rozas's dissertation study (2004) of thirteen women undergraduate participants in a race or ethnicity dialogue at Mount Holyoke College reported that features of intergroup dialogue such as structured activities, group composition, and frequency of contact affected students' learning. Students reported that structured activities helped ease intergroup anxiety and foster equality and cooperativeness in the situation: "I really liked the structured activities . . . because then I felt less [conscious] of myself and it was everyone participating all at once" (p. 5). A balanced composition of members of the two groups in dialogue was also an important condition for equalizing status in the group. Some students' comments identified the lack of such balance as contributing to less positive group interactions and more disconnection. On the other hand, because the contact was regular and sustained over a semester, feelings of connectedness and emotional closeness developed over time: "We're talking about how we feel, but at the same time, we're bonding because of our experiences and talked about these things for weeks" (p. 6).

A retrospective evaluation of University of Maryland participants in six-week intergroup dialogues found that students rated the importance of certain IGD features—a small-group setting, guidelines for interaction, competent facilitators, and diversity in the group—higher than weekly reflection papers and readings (Nagda, Balon, Hernandez-Morales, and Bouis, 2003). Additionally, students of color rated the importance of all conditions higher than white students, but especially significant were guidelines and facilitators. Facilitators' competencies—supportiveness, encouraging behaviors, challenge, and so on—were rated high by all participants, but students of color rated all these competencies much higher than did white students. Subsequent correlation analyses relating outcomes to these conditions showed that (1) for students of color, the small-group setting and diversity in the group showed significant positive correlations with relationship-building outcomes; (2) white students showed a positive correlation between group guidelines and bridge building; and (3) students of color showed significant correlations between action outcomes and all facilitator competencies. The main lesson from these correlation analyses is that the educational design features such as group composition and facilitator competencies are related to relationship building and action outcomes, respectively, but are significant only for students of color.

These two studies begin to point to evidence that the IGD conditions supporting facilitated and structured interactions are important in creating the context for engagement across differences, even when such engagement may look different across groups.

Teaching and Learning Processes in Intergroup Dialogue
In the classroom study of the same social work course reviewed above, Nagda, Kim, and Truelove (2004) applied Dovidio and other's model (2004) of interventions and outcomes in antibias education to intergroup dialogue. The heart of the model looks at the question of how interventions lead to outcomes through intervening psychological processes. Using a pretest/posttest design in their study of social welfare majors, Nagda, Kim, and Truelove determined that the lecture and IGD components of a course positively affected students' motivation for bridging differences, which had an impact on students' value of the importance of taking actions and their confidence in taking actions—self-directed prejudice reduction and other-directed promotion of diversity.

A second study of students in the introductory course (Intergroup Relations and Conflict) mentioned earlier (Lopez, Gurin, and Nagda, 1998) also used a pretest/posttest design but without a control group to assess the influence of varied educational methodologies on student learning: content-focused pedagogy (lectures and readings) and process-focused or active learning pedagogy (experiential activities and reflective journals). Students' ratings of the importance of both these learning methods predicted greater structural attributions for racial and ethnic inequalities and endorsement for actions. Active learning, however, alone predicted endorsement of institutional or societal action to counter inequality and injustice.

Yeakley (1998) explored ways in which affective processes in intergroup dialogues influence change in participants' perceptions, attitudes, and levels of understanding toward members of a different social identity group. In-depth interviews were conducted with fourteen undergraduates who participated in a peer-facilitated semester-long intergroup dialogue. Using a grounded theory approach, Yeakley determined that sharing personal experiences in the dialogue helped lead to outcomes such as increased comfort with difference, increased connectivity across group boundaries, enhanced understanding of different perspectives, and greater intergroup understanding (understanding of participants' own and others' personal and social identities). Support for personal sharing involved information's being received with trust and respect (not criticism or judgment), inclusion of different perspectives, and interpretation of this information in terms of both parties' social identities. Yeakley's study was also instructive in specifying some of the potentially negative outcomes and processes of intergroup contact. For instance, limited direct contact often led to stereotyping, and when sharing personal information resulted only in casual conversation rather than further sharing or inquiry, the outcome was increased comfort but little intergroup understanding. When even deeper personal sharing was received negatively (by stereotype, judgment, or criticism), separation, resentment, and disconnection were among the outcomes: "painful feelings related to being stereotyped or discriminated against because of one's social identity led to increased discomfort with, resentment of, and dissociation from members of the identity group that they attributed the experience to" (p. 1).

Yeakley's study (1998) clearly points to the development of communicative competency—that is, the ability to share and explore social issues in public—as a key influence on outcomes. In a classroom qualitative study of a multisection IGD course, Zúñiga, Vasques-Scalera, Sevig, and Nagda (1996), using students' final reflection papers as data, showed that students in a seven-week intergroup dialogue learned how to effectively engage in communicative actions. Themes of voicing, sharing experiences, listening to others and being listened to, and asking difficult questions were found to be outcomes of the learning as well as facilitating further learning in intergroup dialogue. Building on this study, Nagda and Zúñiga (2003), in their pretest/posttest study of students in the race and ethnicity intergroup dialogues, found that students' valuing of dialogic learning was related to frequency of thinking about racial group membership, perspective taking, comfort in communicating across differences, positive beliefs about conflict, and motivation for bridging differences. The dialogic learning components included peer facilitation, structured activities, being able to disagree, sharing views and experiences, asking questions that they were not able to ask before, addressing difficult questions, working through disagreements and conflicts, talking about ways to take action on social issues, and exploring ways to take action with others. This study underscores the importance of the dialogic learning process as distinguished from casual conversation and interaction in groups.

Nagda (2006) further refines the understanding of IGD communication processes. Based on the earlier study (Nagda, Kim, and Truelove, 2004) identifying bridging differences as a psychological process toward actions to reduce prejudice and promote diversity, Nagda asked what the nature of bridging differences is. He found that a set of four communication processes contributed to bridging differences:

1. *Appreciating difference* refers to learning about others and hearing about different points of view in the dialogues.
2. *Engaging self* complements learning about others with sharing of one's own perspectives and rethinking them as part of the dialogic interaction.
3. *Communicating about critical self-reflection* refers to the examination of one's ideas, experiences, and perspectives as located in the context of inequality, privilege, and oppression.
4. *Building alliances* involves relating to and thinking about collaborating with others in taking actions toward social justice.

The first two communication processes reflect well the relationship building aspect of intergroup dialogue, while the latter two communication processes speak to the distinctive emphasis of intergroup dialogue on contextualizing experiences and relationships vis-à-vis social inequality and social change. This study, illuminating a new theoretical component focusing on what happens in the interactional milieu to facilitate bridging differences, expands our understanding of the nature and complexity of IGD communication.

As a whole, these studies on communication processes show that students learn to engage dialogically and that this engagement is linked to a variety of outcomes. Thus, intentional support of dialogic communication across differences through structured and facilitated interactions is critical to the achievement of intended outcomes.

Long-Term Impact of Intergroup Dialogue

Although the research discussed thus far shows promising outcomes and illuminates the importance of some of the influential processes involved in dialogic encounters, we do not know how enduring these changes are over the course of students' undergraduate careers and beyond. Indeed, the dearth of longitudinal studies looking at long-term program effects is an important limitation in this research area in general.

One exception to this general trend is a study of long-term effects that followed students who had participated in Lopez, Gurin, and Nagda's study (1998) described earlier. Both the course participants and their matched comparison counterparts were followed several years later, just before graduation for most students. Gurin, Peng, Lopez, and Nagda (1999) discovered that participation in the IGD program was critical in helping to reverse much of what may be expected attitudes and behaviors of being socialized in the larger societal context of racial or ethnic inequality. For instance, even just before graduating, program participation was related to more positive intergroup perceptions and attitudes for all students (students from privileged and disadvantaged social groups). White and male program participants did not subscribe as strongly to dominant perspectives on intergroup conflict and educational equity as did their nonparticipating counterparts. Students of color and women participants reported more positive views of conflict and more support of educational equity policies than did nonparticipants. In addition, students of color perceived less campus divisiveness and had more positive interactions with white students than did their nonparticipating counterparts. According to Gurin, Nagda, and Lopez (2004), course participants, when compared with the matched control group, also showed greater perspective taking, greater endorsement of difference as nondivisive, greater commonality with other racial and ethnic groups, more positive and less negative conflict ideology, and greater mutuality in learning about their own and other groups. Furthermore, in looking at civic participation in college, course participants were shown to have a greater interest in politics and participated more in campus politics. Beyond college, course participants anticipated helping their groups or community and promoting racial and ethnic understanding more than did the matched control students. The three areas where no differences occurred between the two groups of students were in gaining knowledge about their group's contributions to society, community service participation in college, and influencing political structures after college.

Gurin, Nagda, and Lopez (2004) suggest that participation in the course in their first year in college likely influenced the curricular and cocurricular choices students made in the rest of their time on campus. The program context—intentional and guided learning about social identities, intergroup conflicts, and social change—can be an important alternative to the larger campus culture so as to cultivate more positive views and feelings of intergroup relations. When compared with control students, students in both privileged and disadvantaged groups expressed more positive attitudes and experiences about intergroup life; they more positively valued racial and ethnic identities, found stronger ties with students who were both similar to them and different from them racially and ethnically, and endorsed more constructive ways of working through differences.

A second study that looked at the postgraduation experiences of IGD facilitators is also informative. Vasques-Scalera (1999) conducted a qualitative study of the impact of intergroup dialogue on thirty former undergraduate IGD facilitators from the University of Michigan. Although the study focused specifically on facilitators, most of them had previously participated in intergroup dialogue. Using questionnaires and in-depth interviews as well as content analysis of reports or papers they wrote as part of their facilitation experience, Vasques-Scalera found that several years after graduation, former facilitators reported greater consciousness of their social identities and more complex understandings of issues of identity and difference; increased comfort with their roles as individuals and group members in systems of oppression; greater appreciation of the role of conflict, critical compassion, and empathy in building communities in and across difference; and increased skills in communication, dealing with conflict, and the ability to translate their growth into action. Facilitators described the ways in which the program gave them the tools to do this work and supported them in their own and others' learning. The data also spoke to the power of being part of a diverse, supportive, mutual learning community in which personal, emotional, and experiential learning is nurtured. The long-term impact is seen in the ways in which they continued to draw on their IGD experiences in their postcollege commitments to work on issues of diversity, intergroup relations, and social justice. In addition to advancing their own knowledge and interpersonal relationships, facilitators reported a strong and committed investment in working on these issues in the organizations in which they work and volunteer. The facilitators' narratives also indicated some of the challenges of maintaining commitments to social justice amid worldly environs that were contrary to the IGD experience, namely, a general lack of opportunities and support to continue social justice learning and work.

These studies show that participation in intergroup dialogue, whether as learners or as facilitators, can have long-term positive impact on commitments to pluralism and social justice. The important issue raised here is, of course, the continuing enactment of these commitments and the availability of supportive conditions that were present in the program itself. Given the embryonic stage of research on intergroup dialogue in higher education settings, much work remains to be done in each of the areas discussed above. As the research on long-term effects suggests, a more concerted research effort needs to be undertaken to situate students' experiences in the larger sociopolitical reality of unequal power relations.

Conclusion

Over the last decade, the research on intergroup dialogue in higher education has expanded in its articulation of outcomes. Furthermore, theorizing about and investigating the design features and teaching-learning processes in intergroup dialogue have led to deeper understanding of how change happens in individual participants, what happens in the intergroup dialogue, and how practices can be improved. Future research and evaluation can address the limitations of current research.

Research methods and design. Despite the range of methods and designs used, future research must address limitations in four areas: (1) accounting for self-selection in intergroup dialogues that cannot be fully handled using preresearch or postresearch designs, (2) observational and behavioral data that do not rely solely on self-reports, (3) longitudinal studies to assess whether the immediate outcomes endure over time or latent outcomes manifest later, and (4) what processes and conditions enable sustained outcomes over time.

Educational design features. More systematic study of the conditions of intergroup encounter is needed, given the variations in implementation.

How does the length of intergroup dialogues (seven weeks, ten weeks, or a semester) affect desired outcomes? How does the length of weekly sessions (one hour or one hundred fifty minutes) affect students' experiences in intergroup dialogue? How do independently offered IGD courses compare with intergroup dialogues that are required as part of other courses? How does peer facilitation compare with nonpeer facilitation?

Facilitation. Skilled facilitation is a critical ingredient in students' learning in the dialogues. More research is needed on the impact of facilitators on students' learning and outcomes and on facilitators' own growth and development throughout the intergroup dialogue.

Role of difference and conflict. More systematic study is needed of different approaches to campus intergroup dialogue and different program philosophies. How do different views and approaches to conflict (proactive or reactive, denial or use) affect the outcomes of consciousness raising, relationship building, and capacity building for change? To what extent are intergroup similarities and differences or processes of collaboration or enlightenment and confrontation emphasized?

Attention to asymmetrical power relations. Future research needs to look more carefully at how asymmetrical power relations (such as in racism and sexism) influence the processes, conditions, and outcomes in intergroup dialogue. Further research is also needed to understand how power relations and dominant-subordinate dynamics are replicated or challenged in intergroup dialogue.

Program Development, Implementation, and Institutional Impact

D EVELOPING AND IMPLEMENTING A DIALOGUE PROGRAM requires attending to a range of programmatic considerations. This chapter provides practical information for planning, implementing, and sustaining campus-based dialogue. It also examines potential areas of impact of IGD programs on the wider collegiate environment.

Because intergroup dialogue is relatively new in higher education, the information discussed in the first section of this chapter relies on various sources: print, the Internet, our own experiences, and informal interviews with colleagues and practitioners. Because campus dialogue programs often face similar programmatic issues and challenges, we also draw from the experiences of practitioners involved in Study Circles and Sustained Dialogue in various colleges and universities.

Zúñiga and Nagda (2001) outlined a set of considerations for developing and implementing a campus-based dialogue program. They suggest a number of issues that need to be addressed during the planning phase: philosophical and practical orientation of the program, institutional context, program location in the organizational structure, funding, and linking dialogues to other campus efforts. In the implementation phase, recruitment and training of staff, recruitment of dialogue participants, and program sustainability should be taken into account.

Program Development

The development of a dialogue program entails addressing the following considerations.

Philosophical and Practical Orientation

An important step in developing a dialogue program is determining the philosophical and practical orientation of the program, including the goals, practice principles, and issues that will be addressed. Several paths lead to creating an effective program, and, depending on institutional context, a particular approach might be more successful. Practitioners may wish to consider some of the practice models—Study Circles and Sustained Dialogue—mentioned in the first chapter, as they are also increasingly used on college campuses.

In choosing a path, it is helpful to clarify what issues will be central and the extent to which social action will be an important outcome. This exercise may influence which approach to dialogue may be most appropriate to achieve intended goals.

Dialogue programs continually grapple with selecting intergroup issues on which to focus. In some cases, focal issues may relate to emerging concerns or tensions on campus or in the larger community. For instance, ethnoreligious issues may be more pressing since the events of September 11, 2001. Recent legislative proposals against gay marriage, anti-immigration legislation, reproductive rights, and ballot initiatives against affirmative action have also redirected the focus of some dialogue programs. Although the majority of dialogue efforts focus on social identity–based issues related to race and ethnicity, gender, and sexual orientation, a few initiatives focus on specific questions or issues. For example, the University of New Hampshire Study Circles engaged in questions and topics such as "Are freedom of speech and a nonthreatening environment mutually exclusive on campus? Gender, power, and difference at UNH," and "University or polyversity? The promise of conflict in the UNH community." At Manhattan College, a Study Circle focused around the question of values and which ones are on the "endangered list" (Mallory and Thomas, 2003).

Institutional Context and Location

An important aspect of context is the impetus for starting a program, which has implications for the location of and infrastructure for offering dialogues. For instance, the degree to which an institution supports new initiatives related to diversity, multiculturalism, and improvements in campus climate will affect program development in many ways. Campuses can start dialogue programs in various ways:

A faculty or staff member initiates the effort. For example, a faculty member at the University of Wisconsin–Parkside participated in community-wide Study Circles and thought the campus would benefit from a similar program.

Students, staff, or faculty members propose the need to explore tensions on campus. For example, at the University of Maryland, College Park, the Student Intercultural Learning Center (part of the Office of Human Relations Programs) established an IGD program in direct response to students' stated need. Students wanted facilitated opportunities to come together to talk across various dimensions of difference so they could explore intragroup and intergroup tensions, forge cross-group relationships, and build community (Clark, 2002).

One or a string of critical social identity–based incidents occur on campus. For example, at Colorado College, an insensitive April Fool's edition of the college paper sparked the desire for a Sustained Dialogue (J. Owens, personal communication, May 12, 2005).

The program structures used to implement dialogues also vary across campuses, whether they are implementing similar or different models of dialogues. Four main structures are possible:

Stand-alone efforts usually offer dialogues for academic credit and draw students from the entire student body (Iowa State University, University of Massachusetts Amherst, Occidental College, Portland Community College, Spelman College, Syracuse University, University of Michigan).

When dialogues are a component of a larger course, students participate in larger lectures with smaller discussion sections and dialogue groups (Colgate University, Columbus State University, Universities of Washington Seattle, Illinois at Urbana-Champaign, New Hampshire).

Dialogues can be a field experience that is linked with courses in the humanities, social sciences, and the professions. For example, a women's studies or sociology class may require students to participate in an out-of-class experience on campus or the community for the particular term of the course. This option provides students with the opportunity to sign up for a cocurricular dialogue group on campus (Arizona State University, University of Maryland).

Cocurricular dialogues are sponsored by student affairs units or student organizations. They offer dialogues in residence halls, learning communities, or for the general student body (Arizona State University, Colorado College, Dickinson College, Mount Holyoke College, Universities of Pennsylvania and Notre Dame).

All these efforts and programmatic structures take shape when decisions are made about where to locate the program in the institution:

Many dialogue programs are located in a university or college administrative office. For instance, on Indiana University's Bloomington campus, Study Circle dialogues on race are located in Residential Programs and Services. The Office of Service Learning offers intergroup dialogues at Bucknell University. At Arizona State University, IGD activities are sponsored by the Intergroup Relations Center, located under the Office of the Executive Vice President and the Office of the Provost. At the University of Maryland, they are housed in the Office of Human Relations Programs, an arm of the Office of the President. At Colorado College, the Office of Minority Student Life works with a student organization to implement a Sustained Dialogue program. Student organizations create and sponsor Sustained Dialogues at the University of Notre Dame and Dickinson College.

In other institutions, dialogue programs are located in a particular school or department. At Occidental College, an IGD course is offered by the Department of Psychology. The Social Justice Education concentration in the Department of Student Development and Pupil Personnel Services of the School of Education of the University of Massachusetts Amherst offers an IGD multisection undergraduate course (Zúñiga and others, forthcoming). At the University of Michigan, the Department of

Psychology and Sociology offers IGD activities through a partnership between the College of Literature, Science and the Arts and the Division of Student Affairs. Because only academic departments can grant credit to dialogue participants, partnerships between the Division of Student Affairs and academic departments are fairly common in credit-bearing dialogue activities. Several departments have granted academic credit to dialogue initiatives: American studies, African American studies, communication, education, physical education, psychology, social work, sociology, women's studies, and general university studies.

Although the institutional location of a dialogue program may depend on a number of factors, including the impetus for the program, the presence of an institutional champion seems to influence the outcome. Institutional champions can establish formal and informal partnerships with academic and administrative units, obtain academic credit, seek funding, or garner institutional backing. Champions are important to dialogue efforts for their ability to advocate, obtain resources, and support the continuation of the program. An institutional champion may be a department chair, a student, a vice president, a provost, a dean of the college, a student affairs practitioner working in residence life or student activities, or a faculty member. The key characteristics of an institutional champion include being passionate about students' learning to work across differences, having the power and resources to influence or make decisions, being willing to lend vocal support to the dialogue program, and possessing the ability to bring together colleagues and students from diverse backgrounds interested in such efforts. Multiple champions located in both the academic and student affairs departments of institutions are ideal.

Funding

Creating and coordinating a dialogue program takes funds, patience, perseverance, and energy (Nemeroff and Tukey, 2001). Given the range of institutional locations and programmatic structures used by these efforts, it is not surprising that the sources of funding for these activities vary extensively across institutions. Although most programs rely on some form of internal funding (in kind, monetary amount, faculty appointment, for example), a few have benefited from external funding. Offices of the provost, dean of students, minority student life, residence life, multicultural affairs, and student organizations and various academic departments contribute to the support of campus dialogue programs in different ways. For expanding the sources of funding of a program, it is always helpful to build collaborations with academic units and gain support from prominent faculty and administrators (Gorski, 2002). States' higher education funds, corporations, and local and national foundations such as Mellon, Ford, William and Flora Hewlett, and Bildner are among the institutions that have granted external funding to dialogue initiatives. For instance, the Words of Engagement IGD program at the University of Maryland, College Park, started with the support of a Pluralism and Unity grant from the William and Flora Hewlett Foundation (Clark, 2002). One of the main challenges faced by externally funded programs concerns issues of sustainability once the funding ends. Securing a stable internal source of funding contributes to program sustainability over time.

Links with Other Campus Efforts

Many dialogue efforts attempt to establish links with other diversity initiatives on their own campus. For instance, some diversity initiatives integrate dialogue efforts with leadership and community development activities in residence halls to prepare students for democratic citizenship in a multicultural society (Zúñiga, Nelson Laird, and Mitchell, 2005). In other instances, dialogue activities are linked to staff development efforts on the campus (Clark, 2003). There also appears to be a tendency for intracampus collaboration to occur on the margins of universities' academic cores (Schoem, 2002). Program leaders who attempt to bridge institutional boundaries without sufficient time, energy, and rewards may become overextended and frustrated as a result. Linking to other university efforts, however, also supports a sense of purpose and commitment. One example of such linking is the Michigan Community Scholars Program, which is built on the intersections of community service–learning and IGD programs in the context of a residential learning community. Students study about community in their first-year seminars, enroll in dialogues, and perform service in diverse community settings (Schoem, 2002). Although the impetus for intercampus collaborations may come from practitioners leading a dialogue initiative, funding from private foundations can play a pivotal role in the development and implementation of multi-institutional efforts. For instance, the Bildner Family Foundation awarded grants to New Jersey public and private colleges and universities to create a comprehensive statewide network of institutions committed to using diversity as a catalyst for systemic change on their campuses. The Sustained Dialogue program at Princeton University and the Sustained Dialogue Campus Network are actively involved in this statewide network (Wathington, 2002). Such involvement not only lends visibility to campus dialogue programs but also allows for cross-institutional synergy, impact, and sharing of resources.

Implementation and Sustainability

Once the philosophy and design of the program have been determined and institutional support is obtained, issues arise of staffing, recruitment of participants, and sustainability.

Staffing

Dialogue program staff perform a variety of tasks, including recruitment of participants, facilitating dialogues or training dialogue facilitators, supporting and consulting with dialogue facilitators, coordinating meeting locations, updating educational materials, and compiling reading materials and other resources. Staff members may have special training in the theory and methodology of intergroup relations or active learning methods and should be competent in intergroup communication and small-group leadership (Thompson, Graham Brett, and Behling, 2001). Currently, many dialogue courses and small programs are primarily staffed by one individual faculty or student affairs professional or by two student affairs professionals. In the case of Sustained Dialogue, students co-coordinate the effort through a student organization. Other programs have five or more staff members. For example, the University of Michigan IGD program has two codirectors, one from the College of Literature, Science and the Arts (LSA) and the other from the Division of Students Affairs (DSA), who administratively staff this program. DSA also contributes an associate director, program coordinator, and administrative assistant. The college contributes a lecturer and the involvement of a senior faculty member. Three to four graduate and undergraduate student interns are also part of the staff (Thompson, Graham Brett, and Behling, 2001). Drawing from both LSA and DSA greatly increases the diversity of potential teaching and training teams. Often it is only by involving instructors from both units that Michigan is able to achieve a diverse composition based on race, gender, and other relevant social identities (Thompson, Graham Brett, and Behling, 2001).

In addition, energetic and continued participation and support from faculty and administrators, both in material (labor and funds) and symbolic (ideas and advocacy) terms, is vital to the long-term sustainability of dialogue programs. These colleagues must be available to help teach courses, provide intellectual as well as programmatic input, and present the academic and institutional face of the program to other members of the collegiate community. Without such support, dialogue programs are likely to be seen as extras, as cocurricular activities minimally linked to the fundamental mission of educating students in the knowledge and skills required for participation in a diverse democracy.

Recruiting Student Participants

College students may choose from a myriad of cocurricular experiences and academic courses. As dialogue activities are relatively new on most campuses, active recruitment of dialogue participants and facilitators is essential. In "Facilitating Intergroup Dialogues," we discussed recruiting and screening facilitators. Recruiting dialogue participants also requires an intentional effort, as students typically self-select into these opportunities. Programs develop a range of strategies to publicize their efforts so they can recruit students of diverse backgrounds, majors, and years in college. Some practitioners send informational flyers to residence halls and academic advisors, advertise on campus radio and television stations, e-mail student groups, present at student groups or courses, and post flyers or send e-mail geared toward specific college populations. For example, flyers in professional schools may promote the value of developing intercultural communication skills for future employment. Another recruitment strategy involves sending letters or e-mails to potential students inviting them to participate. At the University of Kentucky–Lexington, flyers, a Web site, word of mouth, and newspaper ads were used to attract Study Circle participants. The option to register online increased the number of applicants. The most successful method was the advocacy of faculty who allocated class time to promote the effort and offered credit for participation (Stockham, 2001). In general, the most successful recruitment strategy appears to be word of mouth. Asking former dialogue participants to assist with recruitment can be very effective. One practitioner mentioned that students who reported taking their learning into their living spaces were able to motivate others to participate in the dialogue.

In creating a dialogue program, recruiting and maintaining a substantial, diverse group of participants is often a challenge. Practitioners at every institution interviewed set a goal of having a balanced number of participants who represent the social identity groups involved in each dialogue. They also look for diversity in social identity groups. For example, in a gender dialogue, coordinators attempt to have an equal number of men and women from diverse backgrounds (religion, race, and sexual orientation, for example) (Stockham, 2001; Thompson, Graham Brett, and Behling, 2001). A balanced group can contribute to a sense of safety and group solidarity (Anzaldúa, 1990; Pettigrew, 1998). Chesler, Wilson, and Malani (1993) noted that students who are the only or one of a few members of their social identity group in the classroom complain about faculty and students' expectations that they serve as the spokesperson for their social identity group. Balancing numbers is one way to avoid this potentially negative dynamic.

In predominantly white institutions, recruiting students from diverse racial and ethnic backgrounds can be challenging. These campuses may choose to offer dialogues that focus on gender, sexual orientation, religion, and socioeconomic class if they are unable to generate sufficient numbers for a dialogue on race and ethnicity. On occasion, institutions offer intragroup dialogues that focus on exploring a particular social identity (such as white people). In this case, groups aspire to be intentionally diverse, but there is not the same emphasis on having equal numbers of participants from two or more different social groups (Thompson, Graham Brett, and Behling, 2001).

Recruitment tasks vary depending on where the dialogue program is institutionally located and the demographics of the student body. Recruiting participants for cocurricular dialogues that meet weekly or biweekly on a volunteer basis can pose some challenges, depending on the time commitment and incentives involved. Many schools schedule cocurricular dialogue activities in the evening or over dinner in a centrally located residence hall. Credit-bearing dialogues are often more attractive to students looking for an elective or a nontraditional educational experience. Regardless of institutional location, it appears that most programs find it challenging to recruit men from all backgrounds to participate in these activities. We are encouraged that, based on our interviews with practitioners, even at universities that have a small population of students of color, the percentage of people of color enrolled in race and ethnicity dialogues is usually greater than the percentage of students of color enrolled on campus. The dialogue program's institutional location and recruiting pool also influence the diversity of participants. For instance, at the onset of the Voices of Discovery Program at Arizona State University (ASU), participants were recruited only from courses and disciplines focusing on issues of cultural and social diversity (Treviño, 2001). By expanding the recruitment pool to other academic majors and offering academic credit as an incentive, ASU was able to attract a larger pool of students to the IGD activities.

Program Sustainability

In interviews, many practitioners mentioned the challenges of program sustainability in terms of preventing burnout, finding ways to reenergize themselves, and keeping program momentum moving forward. Many practitioners and coordinators volunteer their time to start dialogues. Often other priorities and job responsibilities take over. One practitioner interviewed shared concern about the dialogue program continuing on his campus, as conducting dialogues was not the main part of his job description and other responsibilities were accumulating. Dialogue courses are continually evolving to remain responsive and relevant to students' experiences. Thus, staff members must update course readings each year or semester and be aware of current issues (Thompson, Graham Brett, and Behling, 2001).

Programs that include diversity education, are committed to justice and learning communities, and are interdisciplinary in their study of race, gender, and sexuality are usually marginalized in higher education institutions

(Schoem, 2002). When these programs are relegated to minor status or are defined as tracks, practitioners often feel colleagues do not respect their dialogue work. One practitioner shared the view that her colleagues see dialogues as "touchy-feely," excessively focused on personal emotions and experiences, and therefore nonacademic. She emphatically mentioned how participants' journals indicate otherwise. Yankelovich (1999) also noted that until recently most people assumed there were no particular skills required for engaging in or leading dialogues. Sometimes, senior staff or faculty members assume they can easily run or facilitate a dialogue. These attitudes contribute to the marginality of dialogues and potentially affect the sustainability of a program.

The presence or lack of institutional champions also influences sustainability. Practitioners and colleagues expressed concern about what would happen to the program if they or their institutional champion left the university or college. Would the dialogue effort continue? This is also a concern with student-initiated dialogue efforts that have regular turnover in leadership. Although there is no guarantee of retention of students, professional staff, or institutional champions, continually working to cultivate leaders and supporters and linking to other efforts may help to ease these concerns.

Institutional Impact of IGD Programs

Systematic research about the impact of IGD programs on the wider collegiate environment is not currently available. Drawing mainly from our experience at three different campuses and through interviews with IGD colleagues across the country, we speculate on the potential impact of such IGD programs in several areas: (1) student climate and intergroup interactions; (2) organized student activity in support of improved intergroup relations and antidiscrimination or prosocial justice activities; (3) student service programs, including residence hall practices and relationships; (4) curricular innovations or expansions; and (5) pedagogical practices, especially those of faculty involved in dialogue programs or similar efforts, but also among uninvolved faculty colleagues and peers. Even though much of the available evidence on these matters is anecdotal, it does highlight arenas where IGD practices can be extended and where further research is needed.

One can reasonably expect some carryover of the demonstrated effects of IGD activities on students' attitudes and interactions with broader cross-group student interaction on campus. Depending on the number of students involved in IGD activities, program efforts may also affect aspects of the campus climate generally. At the University of Michigan, for instance, a large number of former dialogue participants have been involved in campus social justice campaigns such as those related to support for the university's affirmative action program. At another campus, many participants enrolled in an IGD course were part of a movement aimed at challenging the university to be true to its mission of equity. Even though participants of color were more active in the leadership of this movement than were white participants, many white participants stood in solidarity in meetings and protests. Several faculty meetings were organized to grapple with the issues raised by the students, including a Speak Out where many dialogue participants spoke and read excerpts from their own writing about their (racial, gender, sexual orientation) experiences on the college campus. The testimonies had a strong impact on the faculty, and many are now committed to diversifying their courses and programs.

The same is true on other campuses. IGD programs have been successful enough on some campuses that portions of the program's philosophy and practice and some of their trained leaders have been used or incorporated into other student programs, including programs to prepare residence hall advisors, first-year orientation programs, partnerships with community service–learning programs, faculty development, teaching assistant training, and student leadership training (Schoem and Hurtado, 2001; Thompson, Graham Brett, and Behling, 2001; Zúñiga and others, forthcoming).

Curricular efforts have also adopted or incorporated dialogue approaches, some in traditional courses and some in entire programs. The preparation of future practitioners in social work and education, for example, have had a broad impact. At the University of Washington's School of Social Work, IGD courses are required of all undergraduate and graduate social work students. Both at Washington and at the University of Massachusetts Amherst School of Education, more advanced courses are available in IGD theory, research, and practice. On both campuses, department-based programs have generated more campuswide efforts.

Some evidence also exists of the overall impact of IGD activities on the campus climate for diversity for students, faculty, and staff. Dialogue approaches, for example, have been incorporated into faculty development programs directed toward building more effectiveness in diverse classrooms at Arizona State University. Faculty members and doctoral students involved in teaching dialogue courses often carry these principles into undergraduate teaching. As they share their pedagogical approaches with colleagues, others have adopted various dialogue techniques in unrelated courses. In some instances, students who have participated in IGD courses have approached their instructors to request parallel efforts be introduced into some of their regular classes. For institutions, dialogue programs create greater awareness of the importance of addressing issues of diversity. For example, one campus is considering dialogue participation as one of the ways students can fulfill a general diversity requirement. Other campuses have developed dialogue activities for professional and administrative staff. The University of Maryland, for example, has piloted several IGD efforts for professional (exempt staff) and support staff (nonexempt staff) to examine campus climate issues facing university employees in the institution (Clark, 2003).

The need to better prepare college graduates to live and work in a diverse society has become increasingly apparent. A growing number of colleges and universities—public and private, primarily research and primarily teaching, undergraduate and postgraduate—are examining and developing curricular and cocurricular campus-based IGD programs to address this need. Interviews with practitioners associated with existing IGD programs suggest that these programs appear to have ripple effects beyond their well-documented positive effects on students. The work of faculty, teaching assistants, and student affairs professionals, the level and quality of students' involvement on campus, the success of diversity initiatives, and the overall campus climate also appear to be positively affected by the presence of a dialogue effort on campus. As these effects are more systematically documented, understood, and enhanced by continued practice and further research, these efforts are likely to continue to grow, to become more sustainable, and to be more effectively integrated with other aspects of the curriculum, with student life, and with other diversity initiatives.

Final Thoughts

W E LIVE IN A SOCIETY RENT BY MAJOR SOCIAL DIVISIONS and social inequalities. People of different races, ethnicities, genders, religions, sexual orientations, and socioeconomic classes often live in different worlds, are ignorant of or cautious with one another, and sometimes engage in serious and sustained conflict. Continuing and, in some cases, rising levels of intolerance and discrimination undermine efforts to achieve a diverse democratic society. Not only are these societal patterns reproduced daily in informal interactions among students on our college campuses; they are often also aggravated by passive and inattentive programs and outdated curricula or faculty approaches. At the same time, students on our campuses are often curious about one another, desirous of crossing social boundaries, and interested in issues of social equality and social justice.

Intergroup dialogue responds to students' concerns and motivations by providing an opportunity for them to explore their own and others' experiences, perspectives, and visions for change. Led by trained facilitators, intergroup dialogues promote sustained and intimate small-group interactions and intellectual and social risk taking. Students share perspectives, ask questions, respond to issues and concerns often ignored or denied, and explore new ways of thinking about themselves, others, and their role in the larger society. This kind of intimate interaction and collective inquiry stands in contrast to the highly individualized approach to learning typical of traditional academic pedagogies and broadens the kinds of educational experience available to college students.

The research evidence on intergroup dialogue that has been presented in this monograph suggests that participation in these activities can increase students' understanding of themselves and others, their comprehension of the roots and operations of structural discrimination and cultural hegemony, and their commitment to take concerted action to create more socially just lives and communities. Indeed, many students who have participated in intergroup dialogues have continued to apply their new understandings and skills in on-campus change efforts and in careers dedicated to advancing social change and social justice.

A strength of intergroup dialogue and other programs that promote dialogic engagement among students is that they can be adapted to different campus contexts. Although IGD programs have been designed and implemented differently on various campuses, they share a common emphasis on skilled facilitation, a form of instructional leadership that supports active, honest, and empathic communication. Most IGD programs blend structured experiential activities and dialogic methods while providing readings and other more traditional forms of intellectual input and exploration.

The effort to find new ways to engage people in meaningful communication and collaboration across social identities and social locations is a key challenge of our time. It requires both the willingness and the commitment to understand group-based differences in identity, life experience, and worldview; to explore common problems, values, and relationships; and to work together to promote change. Unresolved intergroup conflicts represent a danger to social stability, democratic participation, and social justice. Intergroup dialogue promises a significant pedagogical innovation that promotes the development of critical dialogic and emphatic skills and dispositions that a new generation of citizens and leaders will need to build a more equitable, inclusive, and just future.

Appendix: Educational Resources

Intergroup dialogue uses a variety of active, experiential, and dialogic learning methods for students to engage in shared activities, stimulate conversation, foster critical thinking, and deepen dialogues. The first section of this appendix includes educational resources that we have used extensively in our practice. The second section includes resources for training and supporting facilitators. Wherever possible, we have noted additional references for more detailed information about the resources.

Curriculum

When these educational resources are used in the dialogue session, they are supplemented with readings and a set of guidelines for facilitators. Each resource is also integrated into the four-stage design described in "Design and Practice Principles in Intergroup Dialogue"; they are not stand-alone activities. The curriculum relies on connecting each activity and session with specific readings, conceptual organizers, and dialogic methods as well as on the sustained face-to-face interaction of participants and facilitators.

The summary description of each structured activity and dialogic method notes the goals and context, approximate length of time based on a two-hour session, and other supporting materials. The resources, with the exception of "Methods for Deepening the Conversation," are listed in order of use in the four-stage IGD curriculum. A brief description of each stage precedes the respective resources. Resources in "Methods for Deepening the Conversation" are presented separately because they are relevant for all stages of intergroup dialogue.

Stage 1—Group Beginnings: Forming and Building Relationships

Weaving content and process objectives, concepts, and structured activities in this stage supports the IGD goals of relationship building and building the capacity for sustained dialogue. The sessions in this stage focus on exploring the reasons for talking with others about specific intergroup issues and acquiring dialogue skills. We engage the students in exploring why it is important to talk about race, gender, socioeconomic class, or sexual orientation, for example, on the college campus as well as clarifying what dialogue is in relation to other forms of communication.

Why Talk About Race/Ethnicity, Gender, or . . . ? This structured activity supports participants' beginning to explore why it may be important to engage in conversations about race, ethnicity, gender, religion, sexual orientation, and other socially constructed group differences on a college campus (Fox, 2001; Tatum, 1997; Zúñiga, Cytron-Walker, and Kachwaha, 2004). For example, in a dialogue about race and ethnicity, participants may be asked to consider the following question during the second half of the first session: "Why may it be valuable for white people, multiracial people, and people of color to talk about race and ethnicity?" This activity usually elicits a range of responses from participants. Facilitators can help the group identify similarities and differences in perspective and build some shared understanding about why dialogue across differences is needed. When first asked, participants may not be able to articulate their reasons clearly. It may be easier for participants first to write their thoughts on an index card, then share key highlights with another individual and then the large group. We usually allocate approximately thirty minutes for this activity.

Dialogue and Debate. This structured activity helps participants distinguish between dialogue and debate, highlighting the value of dialogue as a form of communication. Because most participants do not have firsthand experience with dialogic communication, we use this activity during the first or second session. Participants brainstorm key characteristics of dialogue and of debate. To help ground the discussion, participants recall a time they witnessed or participated in a dialogue or a debate and describe their reactions to that experience (including thoughts, feelings, and behaviors). A conceptual organizer that distinguishes "dialogue and debate" (Study Circles Resource Center, 1997) is used to further clarify goals, characteristics, and skills involved in each form of communication. Participants are encouraged to be mindful of the purpose and the skills that support dialogue as they communicate in the group in upcoming sessions. We usually allocate thirty minutes for this activity.

Building Blocks of Dialogue. This minilecture introduces participants to the conceptual organizer entitled "building blocks of dialogue" after clarifying the difference between dialogue and debate (Nagda, 2001). The building blocks of dialogue are suspended judgment, deep listening, identified assumptions, and reflection and inquiry (Bohm, 1990). In dialogue, natural judgments are suspended to hear each other (Weiler, 1994). This practice encourages deep listening, which requires our full attention and presence. Identifying assumptions clears up misconceptions, while reflection and inquiry encourage inward reflection and asking questions that build on those reflections. Participants are asked to keep these building blocks of dialogue in mind and to find ways of embodying them during dialogue conversations. Participants further their understanding of this conceptual organizer as they read Weiler's interview with Linda Tuerfs (1994) in preparation for the skillbuilding segment scheduled in the upcoming session. We allocate fifteen to twenty minutes for this minilecture.

Stage 2—Exploring Differences and Commonalities of Experience

The primary focus of this stage is exploring social identity–based experiences and concerns in the context of systems of privilege and power. The interplay of content and process objectives, concepts, and structured activities supports both aspects of consciousness raising—developing social identity awareness and social systems knowledge—as well as relationship building in and across social identity groups. In this stage, students may also begin to identify actions they can take as part of an action project assignment aimed at strengthening individual and collective capacities for collaboration across differences. In structuring the sessions, we may start with concepts and activities that encourage personal and social identity–based explorations (for example, cultural chest, fishbowl), structure a discussion of terminology, and conclude with an activity that helps illustrate person-structure dynamics (such as web of oppression) using generative discussion methods (Brookfield and Preskill, 2005).

Cultural Chest. This structured activity invites participants to explore their multiple social identities through story telling (Motoike and Monroe-Fowler, n.d.). They reflect on and speak about the significance of a range of social identities that affect their lives, including the ones that are the foci of the dialogue. Because the cultural chest emphasizes story telling and speaking and listening, this activity often deepens the level of sharing and relationship building in the group. We usually facilitate this activity in the third or fourth session after participants have generated guidelines for participation to help them be more open and honest with each other. In preparation for this activity, participants complete a written assignment, read testimonials from multiple social identity perspectives (Alvarez, 1993; Atkins Bowman and Buford, 2000; Staples, 1997; Wellman, 1996), and bring a cultural chest containing three objects that are personally significant in connection to three of their salient social identities (including the one that is the main focus of the intergroup dialogue).

During the cultural chest activity, each participant and facilitator is allotted an amount of time to describe the objects and tell the stories associated with the objects inside the cultural chest while everyone else in the group actively listens. Once everyone has had a chance to share, this activity is carefully debriefed using some of the phases of debriefing described in "Debriefing Learning Activities" in this appendix. Possible topics of conversation that may ensue include commonalities and differences in participants' salient privileged and targeted social identities, visible and invisible social identities, the difference between a significant identity and a salient identity, and the role society plays in encouraging or silencing the voicing of particular social identities. We usually allocate eighty to one hundred minutes for this activity.

Terminology Activity. This structured activity supports generative discussions (Wink, 2005) of concepts and terminology that may be relevant to explore near the beginning of an IGD experience. This activity is important because participants (and facilitators) often attribute different meanings to a key concept or term based on their life experiences or social identities (Wijeyesinghe, Griffin, and Love, 1997; Zúñiga, Cytron-Walker, and

Kachwaha, 2004). Clarifying and searching for shared and conflicted meaning is essential in dialogues across differences. We find it useful to schedule this activity in the third or fourth session to help participants recognize that there are different ways of defining terms, with no one definition being necessarily right or wrong.

In preparation for this activity, participants create working definitions of several terms based on their own knowledge, experience, and assigned readings. This activity involves a two-step procedure. In the first step, participants divide into three small groups and create working definitions of one of the following terms: prejudice, discrimination, oppression. Then they present their definitions to the entire group. In the second step, as a large group, participants brainstorm the meanings for the second set of terms. For example, in a dialogue about race and ethnicity, it may be helpful to clarify the meaning of race, ethnicity, racism, and white supremacy. Recording the suggested definitions on newsprint sheets labeled with each term encourages the group to discuss the meaning and identify the underlying assumptions of the proposed definitions and to address any questions about them. The facilitator summarizes the themes, acknowledging that these working definitions will likely evolve as the dialogue progresses. The facilitator also stresses the importance of clarifying the meaning attached to a term or concepts before assuming there is consensus or disagreement. We allocate sixty minutes for this activity.

Fishbowl. This dialogic method supports speaking and listening in and across social identity groups (Fox, 2001; Schoem, Zúñiga, and Nagda, 1993; Yeskel and Leondar-Wright, 1997). It also can be helpful in allowing a particular subgroup in the dialogue to have the floor. A fishbowl relies on an inner circle and an outer circle. Members of one subgroup sit in the center of the room in an inner circle while the other members of the dialogue group sit outside it. Members of the inner circle address a predesigned question or explore a particular intergroup issue or concern for a specified amount of time. Participants in the outer circle listen attentively without interrupting or asking questions and later paraphrase something they heard a member of the inner circle say. Then, groups of participants switch locations (Griffin and Harro, 1997), and a question or topic is posed to the new inner circle. This activity can then be carefully debriefed using some of the phases of debriefing described in "Debriefing Learning Activities" in this appendix.

This dialogic method is used in a variety of ways. When social identity–based affinity groups precede a fishbowl, participants in the inner circle belong to the same social identity group (for example, women, white people). In this instance, the fishbowl provides a format for sharing experiences or concerns with another affinity group. During sessions addressing hot topics, fishbowl structures are also used to explore conflicting viewpoints or group dynamics not necessarily linked to social group identities. The time allocated may vary depending on the goal, issue, and time available in the session, but it is helpful to allocate at least sixty minutes for this activity.

Web of Oppression.   This structured activity demonstrates how everyone is affected by oppression. In particular, it illustrates the systemic nature of discrimination, derogation, and oppression against some social identity group and the privilege of others in modern U.S. society (Arizona State University Intergroup Relations Center, 2001). This activity is usually introduced after participants have had a chance to explore their social identity–based experiences and concerns in affinity groups and fishbowls. To support multilevel person-structure analysis, participants brainstorm examples of individual, cultural, and institutional oppression and then hold the loose ends of a web made of rope. The web has attached labels listing examples of individual, cultural, and institutional oppression built on Katz's conceptual organizer (1978), "levels and types of oppression." Participants read the content of some premade labels. For example, a joke on a web representing sexism might be "What do you call four women at a four-way stop? Eternity" and an example of a law on a web representing heterosexism might be the Defense of Marriage Act. All the examples on the web refer to one particular form of oppression.

Once a few examples are read aloud, participants generate other examples of oppression in society. A discussion develops about why these examples are represented on a web and how the individual examples connect. Participants also discuss how each person is influenced by this system and think of ways that they can stop supporting the status quo.

In wrapping up the activity, facilitators help summarize, noting that everyone is affected by oppression, that all these manifestations support a larger integrated system, and that systems of oppression overlap or are interconnected. If time allows, the facilitator may invite participants to give examples related to other systems of advantage and disadvantage. Reminding participants that social systems can be changed serves as a catalyst for taking actions. It is often an important reminder, as the web activity can leave participants feeling frustrated or discouraged (see "Action Project Assignment" in this appendix). We allocate sixty to seventy-five minutes for this activity. (For a more detailed description of how to make the web and how to facilitate this activity, visit http://www.asu.edu/irc.)

Stage 3—Exploring and Dialoguing About Hot Topics

This stage invites participants to actively explore their perspectives on controversial or hot button issues. Topics commonly selected (by students, facilitators, or both) include interracial relations, relationships between men and women, reverse discrimination, media and gender roles, racial profiling, religion and sexuality, immigration, and safety on campus. Readings, discussion questions, structured activities, and dialogic methods are woven together to support the process and content of these conversations. As participants explore conflicting sentiments, experiences, and viewpoints, they are challenged to spotlight some of the interpersonal, group, institutional, cultural, and historical factors that give rise to intergroup tensions. Participants learn to explore these controversial issues from multiple perspectives (including from the perspective of the other social identity group in the dialogue) and prevailing societal power dynamics. Learning to build, communicate, and sustain honest and reciprocal relationships while working with and across differences and conflicts is a key challenge for participating in this stage. To structure these conversations, facilitators rely on readings, statistics, dialogue methods, and structured activities to help get the conversation started. Questioning methods and active dialogue facilitation methods are used to stimulate cognitive and affective perspectives to deepen the conversation.

We describe below six quick methods to get conversations started about sensitive issues. We also describe two structured activities that can be used to stimulate dialogue about controversial issues and a method for participants to process and analyze the quality of the dialogue during a given session.

Although the content and readings of each hot topic differ, the dialogue methods and structured activities presented in this section can be adapted to most hot topics.

Getting Conversations Started.   Opening conversations can sometimes be challenging, particularly if the topic is perceived as controversial or a polarized atmosphere was created during the previous session (Brookfield and Preskill, 2005). One helpful method is to bring participants' attention to particular content or a question. Some methods support thinking about the topic, while others promote an affective response. They can also encourage a generative, democratic process where everyone may share his or her experiences and opinions. The following discussion methods described by Brookfield and Preskill (1999, 2005) can be helpful as quick dialogue starters:

Sentence completion. Participants finish an incomplete sentence such as "My gut reaction to this topic is . . . " or "The article that affected me most was . . . ". Facilitators encourage participants to ask each other questions about their responses.

Shocking statement. Facilitators read a strong, shocking statement or quote from a famous person that may challenge many participants' experiences or beliefs. Participants start the dialogue by talking about how they interpret and what they think about the statement.

Recall a critical incident or experience. Often participants feel detached from discussions because they do not think the discussion relates to them. Facilitators start the discussion with participants' recalling and then presenting a memory or experience related to or with the topic.

Circle of voices. Four or five participants form a circle and are allocated three minutes of silence to think about what they want to say about the issue of the day or posed question. Once the circle of voices begins, each participant has three minutes of uninterrupted time to speak. Everyone else actively listens. After the circle of voices is complete, the discussion opens to everyone.

Hat full of quotes. Before the session, facilitators type multiple copies of four or five passages or quotes from the assigned readings on separate sheets. At the beginning of the session, sheets are placed in a container and participants choose a sheet. Participants think about the quotes, read their quote aloud, and comment on it.

E-mail questions. After participants complete any assigned readings and before the next session, they generate questions about the hot topic and e-mail them to facilitators. Facilitators use the questions to help structure the session.

Once the conversations get going, facilitators can use questioning methods to probe and further deepen the conversation that ensues from these dialogue starters.

Gallery Walk. This structured activity prompts participants to reflect and inquire on controversial or complex intergroup issues (Brooks-Harris and Stock-Ward, 1999; Wijeyesinghe, Griffin, and Love, 1997). Pictures, quotes, statistics, or participant-generated data relevant to the selected topic are displayed around the room. Participants circle the gallery in silence or in pairs. After all participants have looked at the entire gallery, they share reactions, either verbally or by creating another gallery opportunity where participants write reactions and questions on sticky note paper and place them next to the appropriate images. Participants recircle the gallery and read everyone's responses. Facilitators then debrief participants, using some of the phases described in "Debriefing Learning Activities" in this appendix). A sample hot topic that incorporates this method is body image in the media, for which the gallery displays magazine depictions of body images. A gallery about immigration consists of participant-generated examples of social, economic, and historical factors that influence various perspectives on immigration. In the hot topic of body image, a possible dialogue may arise around the impact of media images on gender roles, relationships, health, and self-esteem. For immigration, a conversation may develop about the causes and effects of immigration, immigrants' rights, workers' rights, and the policy debates concerning illegal immigrants and immigration. Timely use of questioning methods can further and deepen the conversation that evolves from the gallery walk. We allocate sixty minutes for this activity.

Take a Stand. This structured activity clarifies values and provides a format for stimulating sharing and dialogue about a hot issue (Lesbian–Gay Male

Program Office, 1993). The activity provides an opportunity to take risks and to explore similar and different perspectives on a particular issue by asking participants to respond to statements. This activity can be performed in two ways: the statements can be read in silence followed by debriefing and dialogue, or a dialogue can follow each statement. The former will take ten to twenty minutes, and the latter will need at least ten minutes for each statement. In preparation for this activity, participants read articles expressing various viewpoints of the hot topic addressed. The activity is called "take a stand" because it involves publicly owning one's thoughts or feelings about a series of statements along a continuum of comfortable to uncomfortable. A purposely nonevaluative statement is read, and participants place themselves along the continuum based on their gut reactions. For example, possible topics for a session focusing on race and racism on campus might include need-based financial aid, reverse discrimination, racial profiling, special-interest housing, sport mascots (or official logos), or affirmative action. Once participants distribute themselves along the continuum, a few are asked to share their reason for standing in a particular place. Then the next statement is read, and the procedure continues, leaving time for careful debriefing, using some of the phases of debriefing described in "Debriefing Learning Activities." For instance, when discussing various aspects of special-interest housing, including how it helps some students feel safe and others feel excluded on campus, participants may discover aspects of campus climate and society that help foster feelings of comfort and exclusion. The conversation may focus on the limited support students of color experience on campus, particularly from faculty, police enforcement practices, financial aid, and so on. Timely use of questioning methods can further and deepen the conversation started by this exercise.

Dialogue About the Dialogue.   This structured activity creates an opportunity to reflect on the quality of the dialogue process and to raise buried concerns and feelings (Marshak and Katz, 1999; Zúñiga, Cytron-Walker, and Kachwaha, 2004). Even though participants and facilitators may actively work toward creating an open, honest, and reciprocal IGD environment, hidden emotions, thoughts, fears, and needs related to intrapersonal, group, intragroup, or intergroup dynamics may need to surface to deepen the conversation. This activity can be used any time a group faces roadblocks in the dialogue process, although it typically is scheduled right after the first or second hot topic session during Stage 3. Doing so helps identify any covert dynamics that may be stifling the dialogue process. A conversation ensues based on questions that may include How are we communicating as a group? What is working? What is getting in the way? Are there any particular dynamics or tensions that you felt or saw during this session or other sessions that are affecting your ability to participate fully? What are some ways we are using dialogic skills? What are some ways we are not? The discussion that emerges from these questions not only encourages participants to identify any underlying dynamics but also to link them to dynamics in society. Some common patterns that are seen in the dialogue include men dominating the conversation while women politely let others talk before them, white people being less vocal when talking about personal experiences with race, and the ease with which participants move into debate mode. Once dynamics are identified, participants engage in an open discussion of how they affect individuals in the group and the group as a whole. The group also decides whether, how, and what to change or work on with regard to the group's dynamics. Toward the end of this conversation, it is helpful to revisit the group process guidelines developed by participants in the first or second session. Participants can reread the guidelines and suggest additional ones to include. Depending on the challenges facing a particular group, this activity can run from thirty minutes to the entire session. Again, timely use of questioning methods can further and deepen the conversation that evolves from a dialogue about the dialogue.

Stage 4—Action Planning and Alliance Building

This stage shifts the focus of the dialogue from exploring hot topics to action planning and alliance building. The IGD goal of strengthening individual and collective capacities to promote social justice is prominent in this stage. The final session also includes activities for ending the dialogue experience. We describe below two of the activities included in the educational design: an action planning/action continuum activity and an action project assignment.

Action Planning and Action Continuum.　This structured activity helps participants think of concrete ways to continue to take action or to take action in the future (Wijeyesinghe, Griffin, and Love, 1997). Participants identify three actions they are willing to take to challenge injustice. They partner with someone else to share their ideas, ask questions, identify the support needed to carry out these actions, and create a time line for implementation. To help participants think of possible types of actions and where they can act, two cognitive organizers—spheres of influence (Goodman and Schapiro, 1997) and the action continuum (Wijeyesinghe, Griffin, and Love, 1997)—can be introduced, especially if they were not introduced earlier. The spheres of influence create a framework of arenas to act in, including in oneself and with friends, family, and society. The action continuum provides examples of various ways one can take action against oppression. Debriefing and questioning methods can further reflection and inquiry, particularly concerning risks and rewards involved in taking action. We allocate forty to sixty minutes for this activity.

Action Project Assignment.   This structured activity motivates participants to incorporate the information, ideas, and skills they acquire during the dialogue. It encourages learning by doing and can be particularly valuable in helping participants move from dialogue to action. This intergroup collaboration project was designed to bring together small, diverse groups of peers to plan and take an action relevant to the issues discussed in their intergroup dialogue (Zúñiga, 2004). This project provides them with the opportunity to practice some of the skills of cross-group communication such as active listening and perspective taking in a real, task-oriented situation. It is not unlike situations they may encounter in their professional, personal, and academic lives. This assignment is introduced in detail right after the web of oppression activity in curriculum-based dialogues. Students complete their projects in a five- or six-week period and give a class presentation during one of the Stage 4 sessions.

With facilitators' support, students design a project in which they take action as a group to educate themselves or others about an issue of their choice to create positive change in the world. An action project might entail collectively writing a letter to a newspaper or public official; holding a workshop, panel talk, discussion group, or film screening to address a campus issue; discussing an educational or cultural program that participants attend as a group; or collectively creating a work of art expressing some aspect of the issue. To help participants assimilate their experiences, they are asked to reflect individually and as a group on what they learned from the process of working together.

Methods for Deepening the Conversation

Debriefing structured activities and dialoguing about content and process are at the heart of the experiential learning process in intergroup dialogue (Nagda, 2001). They are learned skills practiced and honed in the here and now by participants and facilitators. It is during debriefing and dialogue that participants have the opportunity to reflect on their experiences, compare and contrast experiences, ask questions, and generate insight. It is also the most challenging aspect of facilitation because it requires close attention to various nuances of group life, including intergroup dynamics, participants' emotional concerns and reactions, prior planning, and in-the-moment thinking and feeling. The two categories of questioning to foster dialogue listed below—debriefing learning activities and questioning methods—are skills used throughout the four-stage design.

Debriefing Learning Activities

Debriefing comprises three phases: description, analogy/analysis, and application (adapted by Nagda, 2001, from Steinwachs, 1992). Before the session, facilitators prepare for debriefing by making an outline and setting aside adequate time in the next session to debrief participants.

Description. Facilitators begin the debriefing by allowing participants to describe what happened to them. This description phase helps participants gain an understanding of the whole picture. The facilitator might ask, What happened during this activity? How did you feel participating in this activity? How did your thinking and feeling change during the course of the activity? What were your greatest frustrations or successes?

Analogy/Analysis. This phase helps participants to tie the exercise to real-world situations: What were some of the major issues that arose during this activity? How do your experiences in this activity represent real-life situations? What similar experiences have you had elsewhere? How were your experiences in the activity different from real-life situations? What may be some reasons for that? What does that mean? (The facilitator should notice key words and concepts that participants mention.) How do other people see, hear, or feel about that?

Applications.   In this phase, participants consider how they can apply what they have learned to their lives. How might you apply our learning from this activity to situations outside the dialogue group? How might you continue to learn more about what we have experienced and discussed? What are some next steps in learning more about the issues raised? What is one important principle you learned from this activity?

Questioning Methods

Questioning methods can foster reflection, inquiry, and critical thinking. Timely questioning can encourage conflict exploration and perspective taking from multiple points of view. Being mindful of what types of questions to ask and how to go about asking them (logic and sequence) facilitates and promotes critical dialogic engagement. Although some questions may ask for assumptions or evidence, other questions may help the conversation move to the affective level.

When developing questions in preparation for a session, it is important to consider how participants might respond. Davis (1993), Brookfield and Preskill (1999, 2005), and Study Circles Resource Center (2006) offer some helpful tips: (1) order or sequence questions to help participants work through the question (for example, from specific to general, from personal to institutional, from simple [recall an event or definition] to complex [cause-and-effect relationships]); (2) use open-ended questions to probe for how and why, inviting participants to think about their beliefs; (3) ask one question at a time; (4) use questions that encourage participant-to-participant interaction; and (5) balance the types of questions used to foster and deepen the dialogue. For example:

Affective questions. How does this make you feel? What bothers (or excites) you the most about this?

Clarifying questions. What do you mean by that? Could you explain what you just said a bit more? What don't you agree with?

Assumptive questions. What seems to be the key assumption here? What could be assumed instead?

Relational or linking questions. How does what you are saying relate to what was said earlier?

Viewpoint and perspective questions. Can you help us understand the reasons behind your opinion? How might others see this issue? How do the readings help us think about this issue?

Ask for more evidence. How do you know that? What is the basis for your observation?

Cause-and-effect questions. How do the media and religious institutions influence how people feel about this issue? How does the labor market affect the influx of immigrants?

Summary and synthesis questions. How can you summarize what has been said?

Closure questions. What have you heard today that has made you think, hit home, or touched you in some way? What do we need from each other to continue this conversation?

Training and Supervision of Facilitators

As indicated in "Facilitating Intergroup Dialogues," IGD facilitating takes training, supervision, and skills. This section presents a self-assessment tool facilitators complete at the beginning and the end of their training and a conceptual organizer that helps facilitators and supervisors identify group dynamics issues that surface in IGD groups.

Facilitator Personal Assessment Chart

The facilitator personal assessment chart helps evaluate facilitators' competencies and skills and draws attention to knowledge, awareness, and skills one would like to achieve to be an effective IGD facilitator. This assessment chart is often administered at the beginning and at the end of facilitator training. Some facilitators begin training with some of these competencies and skills (knowledge of one's own group's culture and history); some of these competencies and skills are learned during training (social identity development models); and others are gained through the experience of actual IGD facilitation (working with conflict, working in coleadership roles). Completing training and facilitating one intergroup dialogue are not adequate to master these competencies and skills. Facilitators continually gain more knowledge and experience each time they facilitate.

EXHIBIT A1
Facilitator Personal Assessment Chart

Using a scale from 1 (low skill level) to 5 (high skill level) or "dk" (don't know), please indicate (1) where you are now (your current skill level) and (2) where you want/need to be (what skill level you feel is important/necessary to be an effective group leader). In addition, fill out as much as you can in column "C" where relevant.

	A — Where I am now	B — Where I want/need to be	C — How/where I can get support to get to the skill level I want/need
Knowledge of . . .			
• My own group(s), culture, and history			
• Other groups, cultures, and histories			
• Theories and terminology that inform and guide multicultural work			
• Principles and processes of intergroup dialogue			
• Dialogic pedagogy			
• Social identity development models			
• Group development and group process issues			
• Different forms of oppression and "isms"			
• Differences in definition between stereotypes, prejudice, discrimination, and institutional discrimination			
• Ways in which institutional systems of privilege and oppression may affect interpersonal and intergroup dynamics			
• Issues pertinent to the group I am interested in facilitating			
Personal Awareness of . . .			
• Clarity about my own values			
• Internal emotional balance			
• Clarity about my own identity(ies)			
• Impact of my social identity memberships on myself			
• Impact of my social identity group memberships on others			
• My own preferred communication style			
• Impact of my personal style on others			
• Clarity about my status and privilege			

- Clarity about my status and disadvantages
- My blocks (blinders) to awareness
- My own hot buttons or emotional triggers
- My willingness to reconsider/change my own beliefs, attitudes, and behaviors in the face of new information and experiences

Skills to . . .

- Speak freely and openly with people from different groups
- Collaborate with people from different groups
- Disagree and not assume they're wrong and I'm right
- Recognize and acknowledge personal discomfort with certain topics
- Speak and actively listen in public
- Be organized
- Be punctual and on time
- Plan structured activities and weekly sessions
- Respond to participants' journals
- Develop and facilitate a dialogue flow (from setting the tone to getting a conversation started to inviting reflection to asking questions that deepen the dialogue to wrapping up)
- Facilitate a discussion about a controversial topic
- Prepare and deliver short presentations
- Integrate content information when debriefing an activity
- Prepare handouts that summarize historical or contemporary patterns of inequality to ground a conversation
- Work in a coleadership role
- Encourage and facilitate participation from all participants
- Discuss controversial issues
- Work with conflict (as well as identify points of agreement/disagreement, commonalities, and differences during a discussion)
- Challenge others constructively
- Observe and share intergroup dynamics
- Ask for, receive, and incorporate support and feedback
- Give feedback

SOURCE: Adapted with permission from Beale, Thompson, and Chesler, 2001. This framework is in part adapted from a framework for multicultural competency developed by Bailey W. Jackson.

EXHIBIT A2
Key Issues of Group Dynamics in Intergroup Dialogues

Group Issue	The Way It Looks in Any Group	The Way It Might Look in IGD	Some Things a Facilitator Can Do
Membership	• Who's in • How far in • Criteria and procedure for entry	• Segregated seating patterns • Body language • Lack of attendance or lateness	• Total group work • Subgroup work • Shift seating • Informal leader dynamics
Task Clarity and Commitment	• Level of participation • Completion of initial assignment • Shared definitions	• Treat class as blow-off credit • "We also have to write?" • "We also have to read?" • My learning versus our learning • "How many hours do we meet?"	• Prepare for sessions • Assign weekly tasks • Explain but do not apologize for workload • Integrate readings and writings into in-class dialogues
Norms and Rules	• Behavioral expectations and rewards • Informal patterns of relating • Acknowledging and managing differences • Agreement on what is OK	• Seriousness of conversation • Lack of agreement between facilitators and participants • Starting and ending time • Meeting requirements • Enforcement of norms • "Equal" participation across individuals and groups	• Open to group influence within limits • Plural activities • Work and play • Confronting resistance and sabotage such as naming dominant behaviors and their impact on participants

Interaction and Influence	• Struggles with authority and control • Status and power systems • Control of communication • Social inclusiveness and cliquishness • Good/bad "feelings"	• Who's in charge • Resistance to authority • Competition for who's the smartest or best participant • Identity groups stick together or are excluded by others • Historically privileged groups dominate the dialogue	• Clarify and act on facilitation role • Engage participants in group leadership • Encourage/require participation in tasks • Clarify what issues and feelings are important in the group • Identify relationship issues and tie them to historic patterns
Boundaries	• Dealing with other systems	• Academic requirements and personnel • Ground rules and operating agreements • Staying "in here" or "out there"	• Renegotiate membership rules • Redefine tasks
Output and Production	• Task accomplishment • Feeling empowered	• Personal knowledge • Personal and group/intergroup awareness • Interpersonal and intergroup relationships • Shared passion for making change	• Individual work • Group work • Intergroup work • Integration of doable actions into dialogue • Affirmation for positive personal and collective change steps • Mapping next steps to continue and sustain learning

SOURCE: Adapted with permission from Chesler, Kellman-Fritz, and Gould, 2003.

Key Issues of Group Dynamics in Intergroup Dialogues

This conceptual organizer outlines some key group dynamics often found in intergroup dialogues. It can help facilitators and supervisors identify the dynamics occurring in the group and generate possible responses to those dynamics.

References

Adams, M. (1997). Pedagogical frameworks for social justice education. In M. Adams, L. A. Bell, and P. Griffin (Eds.), *Teaching for diversity and social justice: A sourcebook* (pp. 30–43). New York: Routledge.

Adams, M., Bell, L. A., and Griffin, P. (Eds.). (1997). *Teaching for diversity and social justice: A sourcebook.* New York: Routledge.

Allport, G. (1954). *The nature of prejudice.* Reading, MA: Addison-Wesley.

Alvarez, C. (1993). El hilo que nos une/The thread that binds us: Becoming a Puerto Rican woman. In V. Cyrus (Ed.), *Experiencing race, class and gender in the United States* (pp. 35–47). Mountain View, CA: Mayfield.

Anzaldúa, G. (1990). Bridge, drawbridge, sand bar, and island. In L. Albrecht and R. Brewer (Eds.), *Bridges of power: Women's multicultural alliances* (pp. 216–231). Philadelphia: New Society.

Arizona State University Intergroup Relations Center. (2001). *Web of oppression exercise.* Mimeograph. Tempe: Arizona State University.

Atkins Bowman, E., and Buford, M. (2000). Wheel power. In M. Adams and others (Eds.), *Readings for diversity and social justice: An anthology on racism, anti-Semitism, sexism, heterosexism, ableism, and classism* (pp. 356–358). New York: Routledge.

Banks, J. A. (2002). *Introduction to multicultural education* (3rd ed.). Boston: Allyn & Bacon.

Banks, J. A. (2004). Democratic citizenship education in multicultural societies. In J. A. Banks (Ed.), *Diversity and citizenship education: Global perspectives* (pp. 3–16). San Francisco: Jossey-Bass.

Bavelas, A. (1972). Broken squares: Non-verbal problem-solving. In W. Pfeiffer and J. E. Jones (Eds.), *A handbook of structured experiences for human relations training* (pp. 25–30). Iowa City: University Associates Press.

Beale, R. L., and Schoem, D. (2001). The content/process balance in intergroup dialogue. In D. Schoem and S. Hurtado (Eds.), *Intergroup dialogue: Deliberative democracy in school, college, community and workplace* (pp. 266–279). Ann Arbor: University of Michigan Press.

Beale, R. L., Thompson, M. C., and Chesler, M. (2001). Training peer facilitators for intergroup dialogue leadership. In D. Schoem and S. Hurtado (Eds.), *Intergroup dialogue:*

Deliberative democracy in school, college, community and workplace (pp. 227–246). Ann Arbor: University of Michigan Press.

Bell, L. A., and Griffin, P. (1997). Designing social justice education courses. In M. Adams, L. A. Bell, and P. Griffin (Eds.), *Teaching for diversity and social justice: A sourcebook* (pp. 44–58). New York: Routledge.

Bell, L. A., Washington, S., Weinstein, G., and Love, B. (1997). Knowing ourselves as instructors. In M. Adams, L. A. Bell, and P. Griffin (Eds.), *Teaching for diversity and social justice: A sourcebook* (pp. 299–310). New York: Routledge.

Bennett, L., Atkinson, D., and Rowe, W. (1993). *White racial identity: An alternative perspective.* Paper presented at meetings of the American Psychological Association, August, Toronto, ON, Canada.

Bidol, P. (1986). Interactive communication. In P. Bidol, L. Bardwell, and N. Manning (Eds.), *Alternative environmental conflict management approaches: A citizen's model* (pp. 205–208). Ann Arbor: School of Natural Resources, University of Michigan.

Bohm, D. (1990). *On dialogue.* Ojai, CA: David Bohm Seminars.

Brockbank, A., and McGill, I. (2000). *Facilitating reflective learning in higher education.* Buckingham, UK: Society for Research into Higher Education and Open University Press.

Brookfield, S. P., and Preskill, S. (1999). *Discussion as a way of teaching.* San Francisco: Jossey-Bass.

Brookfield, S. P., and Preskill, S. (2005). *Discussion as a way of teaching* (2nd ed.). San Francisco: Jossey-Bass.

Brooks-Harris, J. E., and Stock-Ward, S. R. (1999). *Workshops: Designing and facilitating experiential learning.* Thousand Oaks, CA: Sage.

Burbules, N. (2000). The limits of dialogue as a critical pedagogy. In P. Trifonas (Ed.), *Revolutionary pedagogies: Cultural politics, instituting education, and the discourse of theory* (pp. 251–273). New York: Routledge-Falmer.

Castañeda, C. R. (2004). *Teaching and learning in the diverse classroom.* New York: Routledge-Falmer.

Chesler, M. (2001). Extending intergroup dialogue: From talk to action. In D. Schoem and S. Hurtado (Eds.), *Intergroup dialogue: Deliberative democracy in school, college, community and workplace* (pp. 294–305). Ann Arbor: University of Michigan Press.

Chesler, M., Kellman-Fritz, J., and Gould, A. (2003). Training peer facilitators for community service learning leadership. *Michigan Journal of Community Service Learning, 9*(2), 59–76.

Chesler, M., Lewis, A. E., and Crowfoot, J. E. (2005). *Challenging racism in higher education: Promoting justice.* Boston: Rowman & Littlefield.

Chesler, M., Wilson, M., and Malani, A. (1993). Perceptions of faculty behavior by students of color. *Michigan Journal of Political Science, 1*(16), 54–79.

Clark, C. (2002). Diversity initiatives in higher education. *Multicultural Education, 9*(4), 30–32.

Clark, C. (2003). Building authentic intergroup dialogues on campus. *Multicultural Education, 11*(2), 31–34.

Collins, P. H. (1993). Toward a new vision: Race, class and gender as categories of analysis and connection. *Race, Gender and Class, 1*(1), 36–45.

Davis, B. G. (1993). *Tools for teaching.* San Francisco: Jossey-Bass.

Dovidio, J. F., and others. (2004). From intervention to outcome: Processes in the reduction of bias. In W. G. Stephan and W. P. Vogt (Eds.), *Education programs for improving intergroup relations: Theory, research and practice* (pp. 243–265). New York: Teachers College Press.

Duster, T. (1991). *The diversity project.* Berkeley, CA: Institute for the Study of Social Change.

Ellinor, L., and Gerard, G. (1998). *Dialogue: Rediscover the transforming power of conversation.* New York: Wiley.

Flavin-McDonald, C., and Barrett, M. H. (1999). The Topsfield Foundation: Fostering democratic community building through face-to-face dialogue. In P. J. Edelson and P. L. Malone (Eds.), *Enhancing creativity in adult and continuing education: Innovative approaches, methods, and ideas* (pp. 25–36). San Francisco: Jossey-Bass.

Fox, H. (2001). *"When race breaks out": Conversations about race and racism in college classrooms.* New York: Peter Lang.

Freire, P. (1970). *Pedagogy of the oppressed.* New York: Continuum.

Goodman, D., and Schapiro, S. (1997). Sexism curriculum design. In M. Adams, L. A. Bell, and P. Griffin (Eds.), *Teaching for diversity and social justice: A sourcebook* (pp. 110–140). New York: Routledge.

Gorski, P. (2002). *Initiating a campus-wide intergroup program: Strategies for starting an intergroup dialogue program.* Mimeograph. College Park: University of Maryland.

Gratz v. *Bollinger,* 539 US 244 (2003).

Griffin, P., and Harro, B. (1997). Heterosexism curriculum design. In M. Adams, L. A. Bell, and P. Griffin (Eds.), *Teaching for diversity and social justice: A sourcebook* (pp. 141–169). New York: Routledge.

Grutter v. *Bollinger,* 288 F.3d 732 (2003).

Guarasci, R., and Cornwell, G. H. (1997). *Democratic education in an age of difference: Redefining citizenship in higher education.* San Francisco: Jossey-Bass.

Gurin, P. (1999). Selections from *The Compelling Need for Diversity in Higher Education,* expert reports in defense of the University of Michigan: Expert report of Patricia Gurin. *Equity and Excellence in Education, 32*(2), 37–62.

Gurin, P., Dey, E. L., Hurtado, S., and Gurin, G. (2002). Diversity and higher education: Theory and impact on educational outcomes. *Harvard Educational Review, 72*(3), 330–366.

Gurin, P., Nagda, B. A., and Lopez, G. E. (2004). The benefits of diversity in education for democratic citizenship. *Journal of Social Issues, 60*(1), 17–34.

Gurin, P., Peng, T., Lopez, G. E., and Nagda, B. A. (1999). Context, identity and intergroup relations. In D. Prentice and D. Miller (Eds.), *Cultural divides: Understanding and overcoming group conflict* (pp. 133–170). New York: Russell Sage Foundation.

Habermas, J. (1981). *Theory of communicative action.* (Vol. 1). Boston: Beacon Press.

Hardiman, R., and Jackson, B. W. (1992). Racial identity development: Understanding racial dynamics in college classrooms and on the campus. In M. Adams (Ed.), *Promoting diversity in college classrooms: Innovative responses for the curriculum, faculty, and institutions.* New Directions for Teaching and Learning, no. 52. San Francisco: Jossey-Bass.

Harro, B. (2000a). The cycle of liberation. In M. Adams and others (Eds.), *Readings for diversity and social justice: An anthology on racism, anti-Semitism, sexism, heterosexism, ableism, and classism* (pp. 463–469). New York: Routledge.

Harro, B. (2000b). The cycle of socialization. In M. Adams and others (Eds.), *Readings for diversity and social justice: An anthology on racism, anti-Semitism, sexism, heterosexism, ableism, and classism* (pp. 15–21). New York: Routledge.

Helms, J. (1990). *Black and white racial identity: Theory, research, and practice.* Westport, CT: Greenwood Press.

hooks, B. (1994). *Teaching to transgress: Education as the practice of freedom.* New York: Routledge.

hooks, B. (2003). *Teaching community.* New York: Routledge.

Horton, M., and Freire, P. (1990). *We make the road by walking: Conversations on education and social change.* Philadelphia: Temple University Press.

Huang-Nissen, S. (1999). *Dialogue groups: A practical guide to facilitate diversity conversation.* Blue Hill, ME: Medicine Bear.

Hurtado, S. (2001). Linking diversity to educational purpose: How diversity affects the classroom environment and student development. In G. Orfield with M. Kurlaender (Eds.), *Diversity challenged: Evidence on the impact of affirmative action* (pp. 187–203). Cambridge, MA: Harvard Educational Review.

Hurtado, S. (2003). *Preparing college students for a diverse democracy: Final report to the U.S. Department of Education, OERI, Field Initiated Studies Program.* Ann Arbor: Center for the Study of Higher and Postsecondary Education, University of Michigan.

Hurtado, S., Milem, J. F., Clayton-Pedersen, A., and Allen, W. A. (1999). *Enacting diverse learning environments: Improving the climate for racial/ethnic diversity in higher education.* ASHE-ERIC Higher Education Report, Volume 26, Number 8. Washington, DC: George Washington University, Graduate School of Education and Human Development.

Johnson, A. G. (2001). *Privilege, power and difference.* New York: McGraw-Hill.

Johnson, D. E., and Johnson, F. P. (2003). *Joining together: Group theory and group skills.* Boston: Pearson.

Katz, J. (1978). *White awareness: A handbook for anti-racism training.* Norman: University of Oklahoma Press.

Khuri, M. L. (2004). Facilitating Arab-Jewish intergroup dialogue in the college setting. *Race, Ethnicity and Education, 7*(3), 229–250.

Kolb, D. A. (1984). *Experiential learning: Experience as the source of learning and development.* New York: Prentice Hall.

Lederach, J. P. (1995). *Preparing for peace: Conflict transformation across cultures.* Syracuse, NY: Syracuse University Press.

Lesbian–Gay Male Program Office, University of Michigan. (1993). Take a stand exercise. In D. Schoem, L. Frankel, X. Zúñiga, and E. Lewis (Eds.), *Multicultural teaching in the university* (pp. 323–325). Westport, CT: Praeger.

Lewin, K. (1951). *Field theory in the social sciences.* New York: Harper Collins.

Lopez, G. E., Gurin, P., and Nagda, B. A. (1998). Education and understanding structural causes for group inequalities. *Journal of Political Psychology, 19*(2), 305–329.

Mallory, B. L., and Thomas, N. L. (2003). When the medium is the message: Promoting ethical action through democratic dialogue. *Change, 35*(5), 10–17. Retrieved November 14, 2006, from http://www.svhe.org/files/When%20the%20Medium%20is%20the%20Message.pdf.

Maoz, I. (2001). Participation, control, and dominance in communication between groups in conflict: Analysis of dialogues between Jews and Palestinians in Israel. *Social Justice Research, 14*(2), 189–208.

Maoz, I. (2004). Coexistence is in the eye of the beholder: Evaluating intergroup encounter interventions between Jews and Arabs in Israel. *Journal of Social Issues, 60*(2), 437–452.

Maoz, I., Steinberg, S., Bar-On, D., and Fakhereldeen, M. (2002). The dialogue between the "self" and the "other": A process analysis of Palestinian-Jewish encounters in Israel. *Human Relations, 55*(8), 931–962.

Marshak, R. J., and Katz, J. H. (1999). Covert process: A look at the hidden dimensions of group dynamics. In A. L. Cooke, M. Brazzel, A. S. Craig, and B. Greig (Eds.), *Reading book for human relations training* (8th ed.) (pp. 251–258). Alexandria, VA: NTL Institute for Applied Behavioral Sciences.

McCoy, M., and Sherman, R. (1994). Bridging divides of race and ethnicity. *National Civic Review, 83*(2), 111–119.

McGee Banks, C. A. (2005). *Improving multicultural education: Lessons from the intergroup education movement.* New York: Teachers College Press.

Morrow, R. A., and Torres, C. A. (2002). *Reading Freire and Habermas: Critical pedagogy and transformative social change.* New York: Teachers College Press.

Motoike, P., and Monroe-Fowler, M. (n.d.). *Cultural chest.* Mimeograph. Ann Arbor: Program on Intergroup Relations Conflict and Community, University of Michigan.

Nagda, B. A. (2001). *Creating spaces for hope and possibility: A curriculum guide for intergroup dialogue.* Seattle: IDEA Center.

Nagda, B. A. (2006). Breaking barriers, crossing boundaries, building bridges: Communication processes in intergroup dialogues. *Journal of Social Issues, 62*(3), 553–576.

Nagda, B. A. (2007). *Weaving a tapestry of courage and justice: A resource guide for intergroup dialogue facilitation.* Seattle: IDEA Center.

Nagda, B. A., Balon, D., Hernandez-Morales, A., and Bouis, G. (2003). *Words, thoughts and acts of engagement.* Paper presented at the Intergroup Dialogue Evaluation Retreat Meeting, October, University of Maryland, College Park.

Nagda, B. A., and Derr, A. S. (2004). Intergroup dialogue: Embracing difference and conflict, engendering community. In W. Stephan and P. Vogt (Eds.), *Education programs for improving intergroup relations programs: Theory, practice, research* (pp. 133–151). New York: Teachers College Press.

Nagda, B. A., Gurin, P., and Johnson, S. M. (2005). Living, doing and thinking diversity: How does pre-college diversity experience affect first-year students' engagement with college diversity? In R. Feldman (Ed.), *Improving the first year of college: Research and practice* (pp. 73–108). Mahwah, NJ: Erlbaum.

Nagda, B. A., Kim, C. W., Moise-Swanson, D., and Kim, H. J. (2006). *Empowering education for cultural diversity and social justice.* Unpublished manuscript. Seattle: University of Washington.

Nagda, B. A., Kim, C. W., and Truelove, Y. (2004). Learning about difference, learning with others, learning to transgress. *Journal of Social Issues, 60*(1), 195–214.

Nagda, B. A., and Zúñiga, X. (2003). Fostering meaningful racial engagement through intergroup dialogues. *Group Processes and Intergroup Relations, 6*(1), 111–128.

Nagda, B. A., Zúñiga, X., and Sevig, T. D. (1995). Bridging differences through peer-facilitated intergroup dialogues. In S. Hatcher (Ed.), *Peer programs on a college campus: Theory, training and "voice of the peers"* (pp. 378–414). San Jose, CA: Resources.

Nagda, B. A., and others. (1999). Intergroup dialogues: An innovative approach to teaching about diversity and justice in social work programs. *Journal of Social Work Education, 35*(3), 433–449.

Nagda, B. A., and others. (2001). Intergroup dialogue, education and action: Innovations at the University of Washington School of Social Work. In D. Schoem and S. Hurtado (Eds.), *Intergroup dialogue: Deliberative democracy in school, college, community and workplace* (pp. 115–134). Ann Arbor: University of Michigan Press.

Nemeroff, T., and Tukey, D. (2001). *Diving in: A handbook for improving race relations on college campuses through the process of sustained dialogue.* Dayton, OH: Kettering Foundation.

Norman, A. J. (1991). The use of the group and group work techniques in resolving inter-ethnic conflict. *Social Work with Groups, 14*(3/4), 175–186.

Norman, A. J. (1994). Black-Korean relations: From desperation to dialogue, or from shouting and shooting to sitting and talking. *Journal of Multicultural Social Work, 3*(2), 87–99.

Palmer, P. J. (1998). *The courage to teach.* San Francisco: Jossey Bass.

Parker, N. P. (2006). Sustained dialogue: How students are changing their own racial climate. *About Campus, 11*(1), 17–23.

Pettigrew, T. (1998). Intergroup contact theory. *Annual Review of Psychology, 49*(1), 65–85.

Pharr, S. (1996). *In the time of the right: Reflections on liberation.* Berkeley, CA: Chardon Press.

President's Initiative on Race Advisory Board. (1998). *One America in the 21st century: Forging a new future.* Washington, DC: The Board.

Romney, P. (2003). *The art of dialogue: Animating democracy.* Retrieved September 8, 2005, from http://www.americansforthearts.org/animatingdemocracy/resource_center/resources_content.asp?id=215.

Romney, P., Tatum, B., and Jones, J. (1992). Feminist strategies for teaching about oppression: The importance of process. *Women's Studies Quarterly, 20*(1/2), 95–110.

Saunders, H. H. (1999). *A public peace process: Sustained dialogue to transform racial and ethnic conflicts.* New York: St. Martin's Press.

Saunders, H. H. (2003). Sustained dialogue in managing intractable conflict. *Negotiation Journal, 19*(1), 85–95.

Schniedewind, N. (1992). Teaching feminist process in the 1990s. *Women's Studies Quarterly, 21*(3/4), 17–30.

Schoem, D. (2002). Transforming undergraduate education: Moving beyond distinct undergraduate initiatives. *Change, 34*(6), 51.

Schoem, D., Frankel, L., Zúñiga, X., and Lewis, E. (Eds.). (1993). *Multicultural teaching in the university.* Westport, CT: Praeger.

Schoem, D., and Hurtado, S. (2001). *Intergroup dialogue: Deliberative democracy in school, college, community and workplace.* Ann Arbor: University of Michigan Press.

Schoem, D., Zúñiga, X., and Nagda, R. (1993). Exploring one's background: The fishbowl exercise. In D. Schoem, L. Frankel, X. Zúñiga, and E. Lewis (Eds.), *Multicultural teaching in the university* (pp. 326–327). Westport, CT: Praeger.

Schoem, D., and others. (2001). Intergroup dialogue: Democracy at work in theory and practice. In D. Schoem and S. Hurtado (Eds.), *Intergroup dialogue: Deliberative democracy in school, college, community and workplace* (pp. 1–21). Ann Arbor: University of Michigan Press.

Shirts, G. (1977). *Starpower: A simulation game.* Del Mar, CA: Simulation Training Systems.

Silberman, M. (1998). *Active training: A handbook of techniques, designs, case examples and tips.* San Francisco: Jossey-Bass.

Sleeter, C. E., and Grant, C. A. (1999). *Making choices for multicultural education: Five approaches to race, class, and gender.* Upper Saddle River, NJ: Merrill.

Sleeter, C. E., and McLaren, P. L. (1995). *Multicultural education, critical pedagogy, and the politics of difference.* Albany: State University of New York Press.

Stage, F. K., Muller, P. A., Kinzie, J., and Simmons, A. (1998). *Creating learning centered classrooms: What does learning theory have to say?* ASHE-ERIC Higher Education Report, Volume 26, Number 4. Washington, DC: George Washington University, Graduate School of Education and Human Development.

Staples, B. (1997). Just walk on by: A black man ponders his ability to alter public space. In E. Disch (Ed.), *Reconstructing gender: A multicultural anthology* (pp. 165–168). Mountain View, CA: Mayfield.

Steinwachs, B. (1992). How to facilitate a debriefing. *Simulation and Gaming, 23*(2), 186–195.

Stephan, W., and Stephan, C. W. (2001). *Improving intergroup relations.* Thousand Oaks, CA: Sage.

Stockham, D. (2001). *Combating racism on campus: Study circles at the University of Kentucky.* Retrieved July 30, 2005, from http://www.studycircles.org/pages/success/sucuofky.html.

Strauss, A., and Corbin, J. (1990). *Basics of qualitative research: Grounded theory, procedures and techniques.* Newbury Park, CA: Sage.

Study Circles Resource Center. (1997). A comparison of dialogue and debate. In *Facing the challenge of racism and race relations: Democratic dialogue and action for stronger communities* (p. 47). Pomfret, CT: Topsfield Foundation.

Study Circles Resource Center. (2006). *Facing racism in a diverse nation; A guide for public dialogue and problem solving.* Pomfret, CT: Paul J. Aicher Foundation.

Svinicki, M. D., and Dixon, N. M. (1987). The Kolb model modified for classroom activities. *College Teaching, 35*(4), 141–146.

Tatum, B. D. (1992). Talking about race, learning about racism: The application of racial identity development theory in the classroom. *Harvard Educational Review, 62*(1), 1–24.

Tatum, B. D. (1997). *Why are all the black kids sitting together in the cafeteria? And other conversations about race.* New York: Basic Books.

Thompson, M. C., Graham Brett, T., and Behling, C. (2001). Educating for social justice: The program on intergroup relations, conflict, and community at the University of Michigan. In D. Schoem and S. Hurtado (Eds.), *Intergroup dialogue: Deliberative democracy in school, college, community and workplace* (pp. 99–114). Ann Arbor: University of Michigan Press.

Treviño, J. (2001). Voices of discovery: Intergroup dialogues at Arizona State University. In D. Schoem and S. Hurtado (Eds.), *Intergroup dialogue: Deliberative democracy in school, college, community and workplace* (pp. 87–98). Ann Arbor: University of Michigan Press.

Vasques-Scalera, C. (1999). *Democracy, diversity and dialogue: Education for critical multicultural citizenship.* Unpublished doctoral dissertation, University of Michigan.

Wathington, H. D. (2002, Summer). Bildner family foundation funds a NJ campus diversity initiative. *Diversity Digest,* 12–13. Retrieved November 8, 2006, from http://www. diversityweb.org/Digest/Sm02/Bildner.html.

Weber, R. (1982). The group: A cycle from birth to death. In L. Porter and B. Mohr (Eds.), *Reading book for human relations training* (pp. 90–119). Washington, DC: NTL Institute.

Weiler, J. (1994). Finding a shared meaning: Reflections on dialogue. An interview with Linda Teurfs. *Seeds, 11*(1), 5–10.

Weiler, K. (1993). Freire and a feminist pedagogy of difference. In K. Geismar and G. Nicoleau (Eds.), *Teaching for change: Addressing issues of difference in the college classroom* (pp. 71–98). Reprint series No. 25. Cambridge, MA: Harvard Educational Review.

Wellman, D. (1996). Red and black in white America. In B. Thompson and S. Tyagi (Eds.), *Names we call home: Autobiography on racial identity* (pp. 29–41). New York: Routledge.

Werkmeister-Rozas, L. (2004). *From condition to consequence: An intergroup dialogue process model.* Paper presented at the National Conference of the American Educational Research Association, April, San Diego, CA.

Wijeyesinghe, C. L., Griffin, P., and Love, B. (1997). Racism curriculum design. In M. Adams, L. A. Bell, and P. Griffin (Eds.), *Teaching for diversity and social justice: A sourcebook* (pp. 82–109). New York: Routledge.

Wink, J. (2005). *Critical pedagogy: Notes from the real world* (3rd ed.). Boston: Pearson.

Yankelovich, D. (1999). *The magic of dialogue: Transforming conflict into cooperation.* New York: Simon & Schuster.

Yeakley, A. (1998). *The nature of prejudice change: Positive and negative change processes arising from intergroup contact experiences.* Unpublished doctoral dissertation, University of Michigan.

Yeskel, F., and Leondar-Wright, B. (1997). Classism curriculum design. In M. Adams, L. A. Bell, and P. Griffin (Eds.), *Teaching for diversity and social justice: A sourcebook* (pp. 244–260). New York: Routledge.

Zúñiga, X. (2000). Working for social justice: Vision and strategies for change. In M. Adams and others (Eds.), *Readings for diversity and social justice: An anthology on racism, anti-Semitism, sexism, heterosexism, ableism and classism* (pp. 447–449). New York: Routledge.

Zúñiga, X. (2003). Bridging differences through dialogue. *About Campus, 7*(6), 8–16.

Zúñiga, X. (2004). *The ripple effects of talking about race and gender: Moving from dialogue to action.* Paper presented at the annual meeting of the American Educational Research Association, April, San Diego, CA.

Zúñiga, X., and Chesler, M. (1993). Teaching with and about conflict in the classroom. In D. Schoem, L. Frankel, X. Zúñiga, and E. Lewis (Eds.), *Multicultural teaching in the university* (pp. 37–50). Westport, CT: Praeger.

Zúñiga, X., Cytron-Walker, A., and Kachwaha, T. (2004). *Dialogue across differences.* Unpublished curriculum. Amherst: University of Massachusetts.

Zúñiga, X., and others. (forthcoming). Promoting student, faculty and institutional development in diversity initiatives: Institutional transformation at the University of Massachusetts Amherst. In S. Hurtado (Ed.), *Promising practices in preparing students for a diverse democracy.* San Francisco: Jossey-Bass.

Zúñiga, X., and Nagda, B. A. (1993a). Dialogue groups: An innovative approach to multicultural learning. In D. Schoem, L. Frankel, X. Zúñiga, and E. Lewis (Eds.), *Multicultural teaching in the university* (pp. 232–248). Westport, CT: Praeger.

Zúñiga, X., and Nagda, B. A. (1993b). Identity group exercise. In D. Schoem, L. Frankel, X. Zúñiga, and E. Lewis (Eds.), *Multicultural teaching in the university* (p. 323). Westport, CT: Praeger.

Zúñiga, X., and Nagda, B. A. (2001). Design considerations for intergroup dialogue. In D. Schoem and S. Hurtado (Eds.), *Intergroup dialogue: Deliberative democracy in school, college, community and workplace* (pp. 306–327). Ann Arbor: University of Michigan Press.

Zúñiga, X., Nagda, B. A., and Sevig, T. D. (2002). Intergroup dialogues: An educational model for cultivating engagement across differences. *Equity and Excellence in Education, 35*(1), 7–17.

Zúñiga, X., Nelson Laird, T. F., and Mitchell, T. D. (2005). *Preparing students for democratic citizenship in a multicultural society: Engaging diversity through Project MosaiK.* Paper presented at the annual meeting of the Association for the Study of Higher Education, Philadelphia, PA.

Zúñiga, X., Vasques-Scalera, C., Sevig, T. D., and Nagda, B. A. (1996). *Dismantling the walls: Peer facilitated inter-race/ethnic dialogue processes and experiences* (PCMA working paper #49). Ann Arbor: The Program on Conflict Management Alternatives, University of Michigan.

Name Index

A

Adams, M., ix, 6, 7
Allen, W. A., vii, 1
Allport, G., ix, 6, 20, 62
Alvarez, C., 94
Anzaldúa, G., 83
Atkins Bowman, E., 94
Atkinson, D., 11

B

Balon, D., 62, 66
Banks, J. A., 1, 6
Bar-On, D., 63
Barrett, M. H., 1
Bavelas, A., 45
Beale, R. L., 21, 42, 44, 55, 56
Behling, C., 81, 82, 83, 84, 86
Bell, L. A., 7, 20, 21, 22, 23, 24, 55
Bennett, L., 11
Bidol, P., 27, 47
Bohm, D., 22, 27, 47, 93
Bouis, G., 62, 66
Brockbank, A., 6, 21, 36
Brookfield, S. P., ix, 4, 19, 23, 94, 98, 104
Brooks-Harris, J. E., 20, 22, 23, 99
Buford, M., 94
Burbules, N., 5

C

Castañeda, C. R., 6
Chesler, M., 1, 4, 37, 42, 44, 55, 56, 83

Clark, C., 77, 80, 87
Clayton-Pedersen, A., vii, 1
Collins, P. H., 10, 34
Corbin, J., 65
Cornwell, G. H., viii, 1
Crowfoot, J. E., 1, 4
Cytron-Walker, A., 92, 94, 100

D

Davis, B. G., 104
Derr, A. S., viii
Dewey, J., 5, 6
Dey, E. L., 59
Dovidio, J. F., 62, 63, 67
Duster, T., 13

E

Ellinor, L., 4, 42

F

Fakhereldeen, M., 63
Flavin-McDonald, C., 1
Fox, H., 92, 95
Frankel, L., 1
Freire, P., ix, 3, 6, 9, 19, 47

G

Gerard, G., 4, 42
Goodman, D., 17, 38, 102
Gorski, P., 80
Graham Brett, T., 81, 82, 83, 84, 86
Grant, C. A., 7

Sleeter, C. E., 1, 6, 7
Stage, F. K., ix, 19
Staples, B., 94
Steinberg, S., 63
Steinwachs, B., 23, 103
Stephan, C. W., x, 1, 5, 26, 59
Stephan, W., x, 1, 5, 26, 59
Stockham, D., 83
Stock-Ward, S. R., 20, 22, 23, 99
Strauss, A., 65

T

Tatum, B. D., 1, 7, 11, 21, 36, 92
Teurfs, L., 22, 93
Thomas, N. L., 76
Thompson, M. C., 42, 44, 55, 56, 81, 82, 83, 84, 86
Torres, C. A., 6
Treviño, J., 84
Truelove, Y., xi, 60, 67, 69
Tukey, D., 79

V

Vasques-Scalera, C., 11, 63, 68, 71

W

Washington, S., 55
Wathington, H. D., 81
Weber, R., 20, 25
Weiler, J., 4, 6, 22, 100
Weinstein, G., 55
Wellman, D., 94
Werkmeister-Rozas, L., 62, 63, 65
Wijeyesinghe, C. L., 94, 99, 101, 102
Wilson, M., 83
Wink, J., ix, 4, 6, 94

Y

Yankelovich, D., 85
Yeakley, A., xi, 20, 63, 67, 68
Yeskel, F., 95

Z

Zúñiga, X., viii, x, xi, 1, 3, 5, 10, 11, 16, 18, 21, 26, 34, 36, 42, 62, 63, 65, 68, 75, 80, 86, 92, 94, 95, 100, 102

Subject Index

A
Action planning and alliance building, 28, 30–31, 101–102
Affective questions, 104
Assumptive questions, 104

B
Bollinger, Gratz v., 59
Bollinger, Grutter v., 59
"Building blocks of dialogue" minilecture, 22, 26, 93

C
Cause-and-effect questions, 105
Circle of voices, 98
Clarifying questions, 104
Closure questions, 105
Communication processes, defined, 63
Consciousness raising, 9–12
Conversations
    deepening, 103–105
    starting, 98–99
Cultural chest activity, 94
Curriculum, four-stage IGD, 91–102

D
Debriefing learning activities, 94, 103–104
Dialogue about the dialogue activity, 23–24, 100–101
Dialogue and debate activity, 26, 92–93
Dialogue starters, 98–99
Differences, bridging, 14–16, 69

Differences and commonalities, exploring, 26, 27, 29, 33–35, 93–97
Diversity to justice sequencing, 24

F
Facilitator personal assessment chart, 105, 106–107
Facilitators
    competencies required for, 41–43
    issues faced by, 51–58
    preparing, 43–51, 105–110
    responsibilities of, x
Fishbowl activity, 22, 23, 35, 95–96
Four-stage design of intergroup dialogue, 26–31
Funding, dialogue program, 79–80

G
Gallery walk activity, 22, 99
Goals of intergroup dialogue, viii, 9–18
Gratz v. Bollinger, 59
Group dynamics, 108–109, 110
Grutter v. Bollinger, 59

H
Hat full of quotes dialogue starter, 98–99
Historical roots of intergroup dialogue, 5–7

I
Institutional impact of IGD programs, xi, 69–72, 85–87

About the Authors

Ximena Zúñiga is an associate professor affiliated with the social justice education concentration in the Department of Student Development and Pupil Personnel Services, School of Education, University of Massachusetts Amherst. Before serving in her current position, she was the director and cofounder of the Program on Intergroup Relations at the University of Michigan. Her teaching and research interests focus on pedagogy and diversity, intergroup dialogue, practitioner research, and college student development in social justice education. She is coeditor of *Multicultural Teaching in the University* and *Readings for Diversity and Social Justice*. She consults regularly with faculty, administrators, and student affairs professionals working to infuse and evaluate curricular and cocurricular dialogue programs. She is currently a co-principal investigator for a multi-institutional study to evaluate the impact of intergroup dialogue.

Biren (Ratnesh) A. Nagda is associate professor of social work and director of the Intergroup Dialogue, Education and Action (IDEA) Center at the University of Washington. In 2001, he received the University of Washington Distinguished Teaching Award. In 2006, the IDEA center received the University of Washington Brotman Award for instructional excellence. His research and teaching interests focus on cultural diversity and social justice, intergroup dialogue, and empowerment-oriented social work practice and education. He recently completed a study of community-based dialogue programs and is currently a co-principal investigator for a multi-institutional intergroup dialogue research study.

Mark Chesler is a professor of sociology at the University of Michigan and executive director of Community Resources Ltd. in Ann Arbor. He was one of the cofounders of the Program on Intergroup Relations at the University of Michigan and has helped train undergraduate students for facilitative leadership roles in intergroup dialogue since the program's inception. He is an active researcher, writing on student and faculty responses to social justice and multiculturalism in higher education. He is also active as a consultant with a variety of organizations that are attempting to challenge race and gender discrimination and implement organizational change.

Adena Cytron-Walker is a practitioner of intergroup dialogue and has actively contributed to the development of this practice over the past eight years. She was a dialogue participant and a facilitator as an undergraduate student at the University of Michigan. At the University of Massachusetts, she coordinated the IGD program, trained and consulted with facilitators, and developed curricula to support dialogues across race, ethnicity, gender, and sexual orientation. She is currently working on a curriculum for publication to support gender, race, and ethnicity dialogues in higher education. She works on issues of equality and social justice.

About the ASHE Higher Education Report Series

Since 1983, the ASHE (formerly ASHE-ERIC) Higher Education Report Series has been providing researchers, scholars, and practitioners with timely and substantive information on the critical issues facing higher education. Each monograph presents a definitive analysis of a higher education problem or issue, based on a thorough synthesis of significant literature and institutional experiences. Topics range from planning to diversity and multiculturalism, to performance indicators, to curricular innovations. The mission of the Series is to link the best of higher education research and practice to inform decision making and policy. The reports connect conventional wisdom with research and are designed to help busy individuals keep up with the higher education literature. Authors are scholars and practitioners in the academic community. Each report includes an executive summary, review of the pertinent literature, descriptions of effective educational practices, and a summary of key issues to keep in mind to improve educational policies and practice.

The Series is one of the most peer reviewed in higher education. A National Advisory Board made up of ASHE members reviews proposals. A National Review Board of ASHE scholars and practitioners reviews completed manuscripts. Six monographs are published each year and they are approximately 120 pages in length. The reports are widely disseminated through Jossey-Bass and John Wiley & Sons, and they are available online to subscribing institutions through Wiley InterScience (http://www.interscience.wiley.com).

Call for Proposals

The ASHE Higher Education Report Series is actively looking for proposals. We encourage you to contact one of the editors, Dr. Kelly Ward (kaward@wsu.edu) or Dr. Lisa Wolf-Wendel (lwolf@ku.edu), with your ideas.

Recent Titles

Back Issue/Subscription Order Form

Copy or detach and send to:

Jossey-Bass, A Wiley Imprint, 989 Market Street, San Francisco CA 94103-1741

Call or fax toll-free: Phone 888-378-2537 6:30AM – 3PM PST; Fax 888-481-2665

Back Issues: Please send me the following issues at $26 each
(Important: please include series abbreviation and issue number.
For example ASHE 28:1)

_____

_____

_____

$ _____ Total for single issues

$ _____ SHIPPING CHARGES: SURFACE   Domestic Canadian
                                  First Item $5.00 $6.00
                                  Each Add'l Item $3.00 $1.50
                  For next-day and second-day delivery rates, call the number listed above.

Subscriptions   Please ❑ start ❑ renew my subscription to *ASHE Higher Education Report* for the year 2_____ at the following rate:

U.S.	❑ Individual $165	❑ Institutional $199
Canada	❑ Individual $165	❑ Institutional $235
All Others	❑ Individual $201	❑ Institutional $310
	❑ Online subscriptions available too!	

**For more information about online subscriptions, visit
www.interscience.wiley.com**

$ _____ Total single issues and subscriptions (Add appropriate sales tax for your state for single issue orders. No sales tax for U.S. subscriptions. Canadian residents, add GST for subscriptions and single issues.)

❑Payment enclosed (U.S. check or money order only)
❑VISA ❑ MC ❑ AmEx ❑ #_____ Exp. Date _____

Signature _____ Day Phone _____
❑ Bill Me (U.S. institutional orders only. Purchase order required.)

Purchase order # _____
                  Federal Tax ID13559302   **GST 89102 8052**

Name _____

Address _____

_____

Phone _____ E-mail _____ .

For more information about Jossey-Bass, visit our Web site at www.josseybass.com

ASHE-ERIC HIGHER EDUCATION REPORT IS NOW AVAILABLE ONLINE AT WILEY INTERSCIENCE

What is Wiley InterScience?

Wiley InterScience is the dynamic online content service from John Wiley & Sons delivering the full text of over 300 leading scientific, technical, medical, and professional journals, plus major reference works, the acclaimed Current Protocols laboratory manuals, and even the full text of select Wiley print books online.

What are some special features of Wiley InterScience?

Wiley Interscience Alerts is a service that delivers table of contents via e-mail for any journal available on Wiley InterScience as soon as a new issue is published online.

Early View is Wiley's exclusive service presenting individual articles online as soon as they are ready, even before the release of the compiled print issue. These articles are complete, peer-reviewed, and citable.

CrossRef is the innovative multi-publisher reference linking system enabling readers to move seamlessly from a reference in a journal article to the cited publication, typically located on a different server and published by a different publisher.

How can I access Wiley InterScience?

Visit http://www.interscience.wiley.com.

Guest Users can browse Wiley InterScience for unrestricted access to journal Tables of Contents and Article Abstracts, or use the powerful search engine. *Registered Users* are provided with a *Personal Home Page* to store and manage customized alerts, searches, and links to favorite journals and articles. Additionally, Registered Users can view free Online Sample Issues and preview selected material from major reference works.

Licensed Customers are entitled to access full-text journal articles in PDF, with select journals also offering full-text HTML.

How do I become an Authorized User?

Authorized Users are individuals authorized by a paying Customer to have access to the journals in Wiley InterScience. For example, a University that subscribes to Wiley journals is considered to be the Customer. Faculty, staff and students authorized by the University to have access to those journals in Wiley InterScience are Authorized Users. Users should contact their Library for information on which Wiley journals they have access to in Wiley InterScience.

ASK YOUR INSTITUTION ABOUT WILEY INTERSCIENCE TODAY!

Breinigsville, PA USA
17 March 2011
257825BV00001B/67/P